The
MINDFUL
CBT
WORKBOOK
for Kids

Life Skills to Tame Anxiety,
Handle Big Feelings, Get Things Done,
and Have More Fun

Seth J. Gillihan, PhD, with Ada J.L. & Faye L.L. Gillihan

THE MINDFUL CBT WORKBOOK FOR KIDS

Published by
PESI Publishing, Inc.
3839 White Ave
Eau Claire, WI 54703

Cover and interior design by Amy Rubenzer
Editing by Chelsea Thompson

ISBN 9781683737346 (print)
ISBN 9781683737353 (KPF)
ISBN 9781683737360 (ePDF)

PESI Publishing
pesipublishing.com

Table of Contents

A Letter to Kids

Hello!

I'm really glad you have this workbook. I know it's not easy being a kid. You have a lot going on with school, friends, and your family. Maybe you take music lessons, play sports, or belong to a club. These things are fun, but they're not always easy.

Also, a lot of things are changing when you're young. You're growing, friendships shift, and every year you start a new grade in school. Just when you've figured things out, everything changes.

Plus, sometimes the adults in your life misunderstand you or make mistakes. They also have most of the power and get to make many of the decisions that affect you.

We created this book to help you deal with all these things. The lessons in this book will teach you some simple skills to train your mind, choose the best actions, and decide where to put your attention.

These skills will help you not only now, but also as you get older and face new and exciting challenges. As you grow up, your new skills will grow with you.

I hope you learn a lot from this workbook
and that you have fun doing it.
I am cheering for you!

Seth

A Letter to Parents

Hello, dear parent.

When I've treated young people in my practice, I've always been amazed at how hard the parents are working. They're doing everything they can to help their kids: the mental work of researching their child's condition, the emotional work of dealing with difficult feelings and behavior, the practical work of bringing them to therapy.

If you're reading this book as a parent, you probably know firsthand the challenges I'm describing. I know them as a parent, too, from when my own children have faced common struggles like anxiety and worry. We hurt when our kids are hurting, and we will do anything we can to help them navigate the choppy waters of childhood.

I created this workbook because kids are struggling more than ever as they experience unprecedented levels of anxiety, depression, and hopelessness. This book offers well-tested skills to help your child deal with the many difficulties of growing up.

While the dangers are real, please know that there are lots of reasons for hope. With consistent practice, kids can not only find relief from their current struggles but move toward adulthood with a new set of skills to face all the things that life will bring their way.

With love and all best wishes,

Seth Gillihan, PhD

PS: I've included an introductory guide to mindful CBT just for parents, which includes information about how to help a child who's struggling. You can access it at sethgillihan.com/books/CBT-parents.

A Letter to Therapists

Hello, my friend.

As a therapist who treats kids, you are no doubt aware of the growing crisis among young people. Alarming rates of mental health struggles have brought more and more children to therapy. Now more than ever, therapists need simple and effective ways to help their young clients navigate the challenges they face.

This workbook is intended to meet that need. In *The Mindful CBT Workbook for Kids*, you'll find the best research-backed skills of mindful cognitive behavioral therapy (CBT) in a format that is both substantive and child-centered. Kids will enjoy the colorful images and simple presentation; therapists will appreciate the wealth of resources for use in client sessions, including many worksheets.

This workbook will also help your clients' parents understand the skills their kids are learning and how they can best support the work of therapy.

I know that being a therapist is both difficult and rewarding. We want nothing more than to be of service to those who seek our help, and never more so than with children, whose whole lives are ahead of them.

My hope is that this workbook will make your work both easier and more satisfying as you see your clients benefiting from the powerful practices of mindfulness and CBT.

Wishing all the best for you and the kids you treat,

Seth Gillihan, PhD

Part 1
LEARNING THE SKILLS

In the first part of this workbook, you'll learn what mindful CBT is and how to practice it.

Chapter 1 will show you what mindfulness and CBT are and why they're so helpful.

Chapters 2, 3, and 4 will introduce you to the big skills in mindful CBT, which can be summed up in three little words: **THINK**, **ACT**, and **BE**.

Then in part 2 of the book, you'll see how these skills can improve your life in lots of different ways.

Welcome to Mindful Cognitive Behavioral Therapy

Mindful cognitive behavioral therapy is a big name for some really simple ideas. In this first chapter, you'll learn what cognitive behavioral therapy is ("CBT" for short).

We'll also explore what it means to be "mindful." You'll quickly see why we put mindfulness and CBT together.

A really important part of mindful CBT is knowing that it works, so we'll look at how we know that the skills you'll be working on are helpful. Toward the end of this chapter, you'll learn two of the big skills in mindful CBT: 1) setting goals and 2) solving problems.

In this chapter and throughout this workbook, you'll be using the skills you're learning to deal with things in your own life. Ready? Let's begin!

What Is CBT?

CBT stands for **cognitive behavioral therapy**. You can think of it as **a set of tools to make life better**. CBT can help you:

- Understand what you think, how you feel, and what you do.

- Change your thoughts and actions, which will help you feel better and enjoy your life more.

Let's look at an example of how this works.

Drew's Fear of Dogs

Drew is afraid of dogs. Whenever she sees a dog:

- She *thinks* the dog is mean and might hurt her. (**thought**)

- She *feels* afraid. (**feeling**)

- She *stays as far away* from the dog as she can. (**action**)

These three things—**thought**, **feeling**, and **action**—make something called a **CBT Triangle**.

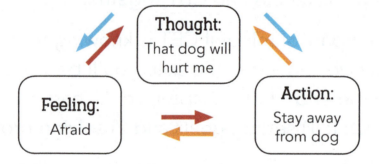

The blue arrows in Drew's CBT Triangle show how her thoughts affect her feelings and actions:

- They make her *feel* more afraid (feeling) because she thinks the dog will hurt her.

- They make her more likely to *stay away* (action) from dogs.

The orange arrows show how Drew's actions affect her thoughts and feelings:

- When she avoids a dog, she keeps *thinking* he's dangerous and would bite her (thoughts), even if he's actually a safe, friendly dog.

- She keeps *feeling* afraid (feelings) of the dog.

Finally, the red arrows show that feeling afraid leads to *thinking* scary thoughts and *avoiding* what she's afraid of.

Now that Drew sees how these pieces fit together, she can use the new skills she's learning in CBT to change her thoughts and her actions.

Together, these changes will help her overcome her fear! When she's less afraid of dogs, she'll also be able to go to fun places she has been avoiding, such as parks and her friend's house.

Now it's your turn!

Think of something difficult in your own life. It could be a worry, a problem with a friend, something at school, or anything else.

You can fill in this blank CBT Triangle with your own thoughts, feelings, and actions.

Then think about how each part of that issue affects the others, just like we did for Drew.

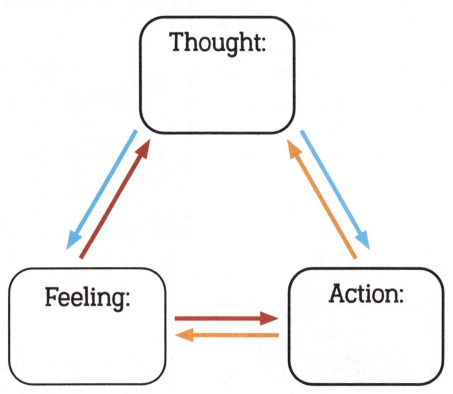

Thoughts ➜ Feelings _____

Thoughts ➜ Actions _____

Actions ➜ Thoughts _____

Actions ➜ Feelings _____

Feelings ➜ Thoughts _____

Feelings ➜ Actions _____

Later in this workbook, you'll learn how to work with your thoughts, feelings, and actions so it's easier to deal with these kinds of challenges.

What Is Mindfulness?

It can be helpful to think of mindfulness as a calm place within you.

It's like the ocean. There may be a lot going on at the surface, like big waves, ships, or storms.

But no matter how rough things are above the water, the water deeper down is always peaceful.

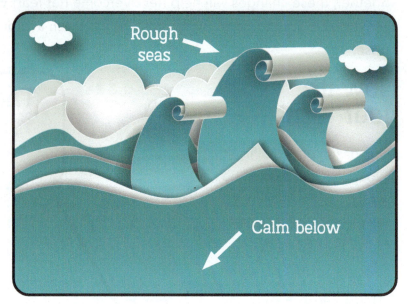

It's the same when there are "storms" in your life, like a problem at home or at school.

It might feel like there are big waves crashing into you. But **there is also a place inside you where you can always find calm.**

Let's practice connecting with this inner quiet for a couple moments right now.

Take a full, gentle breath in, nice and easy, and then breathe out slowly. It might help to put one hand on your heart and the other on your belly. You can close your eyes if you want or leave them open.

Take a couple more easy breaths like that. And just notice how you feel. Whatever you feel is perfectly okay! This is not a test. With practice, it will get easier to find that sense of calm.

You'll be learning lots of ways to practice mindfulness in this workbook. And as you'll see on the next page, mindfulness goes really well with CBT!

Why Mindfulness + CBT?

Let's take a closer look at the CBT Triangle to see why mindfulness and CBT go so well together. This time, we've added mindfulness in the middle.

Mindfulness helps with thoughts. When you find a bit of quiet, it's easier to hear what your mind is telling you and figure out if it makes sense.

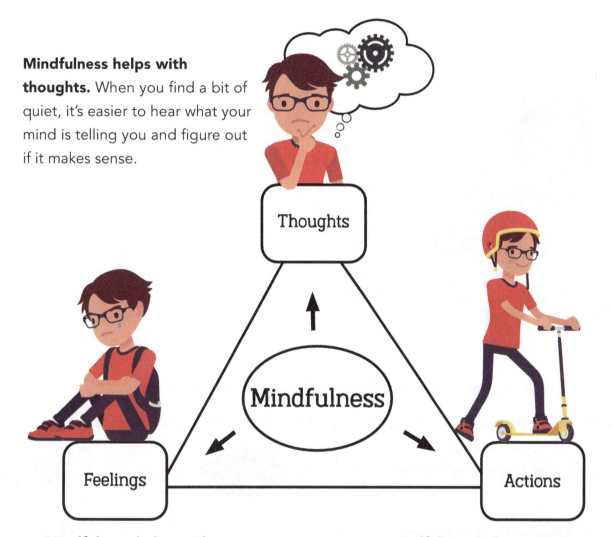

Mindfulness helps with feelings. Difficult feelings are easier to deal with when you drop into that mindful place inside you. The feelings might still be there, but they're less upsetting.

Mindfulness helps with actions. Connecting to that peaceful center inside you will help you choose the best actions. Mindfulness even helps you to be more okay with doing things that are hard or uncomfortable.

Scientists have found that mindfulness and CBT can be powerful together. On the next page, you'll discover more about how we know they work.

How Do We Know That CBT and Mindfulness Can Help?

My favorite thing about CBT is that it can make people's lives better. But how do we know it works?

This question is so important. If we're going to use our time and effort to learn new skills, we want to know they'll be helpful!

Scientists have done hundreds of studies to find out if these tools help people feel better.

First, they find a group of people who want to be in their study. Then the scientists see how they're doing *before* CBT. Next, they teach them the kinds of skills you're learning in this book.

And finally, they see how the people in the study are doing *after* CBT to find out if it was helpful. The best studies in this area compare the group that got CBT to another group that hasn't yet learned CBT.

Most of these studies have found that CBT made a big difference.

When the scientists check in on people who got CBT a few weeks or months later, they usually find that they're still feeling better.

After many studies like this, we know that people who learn and use CBT tend to feel happier, calmer, and less anxious. They also start to enjoy their lives more.

This means you can feel confident that these tried-and-true methods can improve your life! The skills of mindfulness and CBT can help you just like they've helped the people who have come to see me in my office.

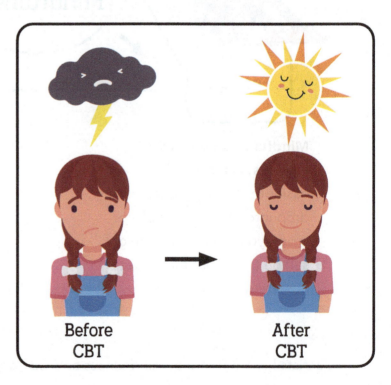

Before CBT   After CBT

The Magic of Setting Goals

The first step in mindful CBT is to choose your **goals**.

You can think of goals as **how you want your life to be better**. Choosing goals will help you get the most out of CBT.

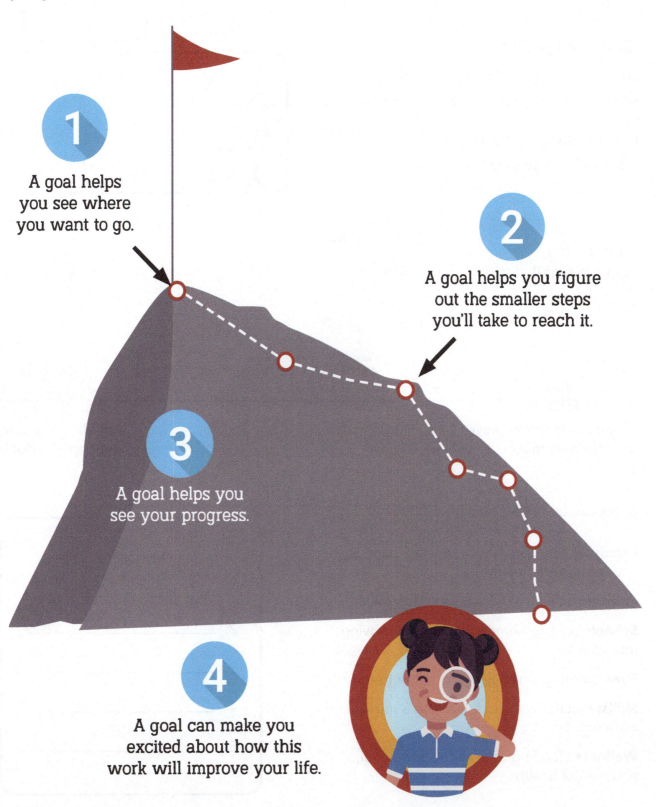

1 A goal helps you see where you want to go.

2 A goal helps you figure out the smaller steps you'll take to reach it.

3 A goal helps you see your progress.

4 A goal can make you excited about how this work will improve your life.

Some goals are more useful than others. The most helpful goals are:

Important to you

The best goals aren't just things adults want you to do. They're things *you* actually care about!

Clear and specific

When you know where you're aiming, you'll know when you've hit the target. For example:

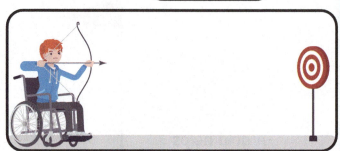

Less helpful goal: Feel better
More helpful goal: Reduce my anxiety

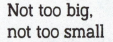

Not too big, not too small

Tiny goals won't improve your life very much.

Huge goals will feel impossible.

Middle-sized goals are exciting and doable.

Goals can be for any part of your life:

Family: Relationships with siblings, parents, cousins, grandparents

Friends: Making new ones, solving conflict

School: Getting homework done, improving attendance

Fun: Learning a hobby, finding time to relax

Skills: Practicing a sport, learning a musical instrument

Wellness: Tending to physical, emotional, and mental health

My goals:

1. _____

2. _____

3. _____

4. _____

5. _____

How to Solve Problems

Some problems are small and easy to solve, like seeing that your shoe is untied and deciding to tie it.

But other problems are bigger and don't have clear solutions. For example, when Charlie moved to a new school, he wasn't sure how to make friends.

For these kinds of problems, it helps to use a **plan** to find the best solution.

That's exactly what Charlie did. He worked through a plan to solve this problem, and now he has a nice group of friends at his new school!

Let's make a plan to solve a small- to medium-sized problem in your own life. It could be an issue at school or with a friend, a problem at home, or anything else.

The first step is to **say clearly what the problem is**.

Next, **decide on your goal**—what will happen to let you know that the problem is solved?

1 **What is the problem?**

_____

_____

2 **What is your goal?**

_____

_____

Steps 3–6 will build a bridge from where you are (1) to where you want to go (2).

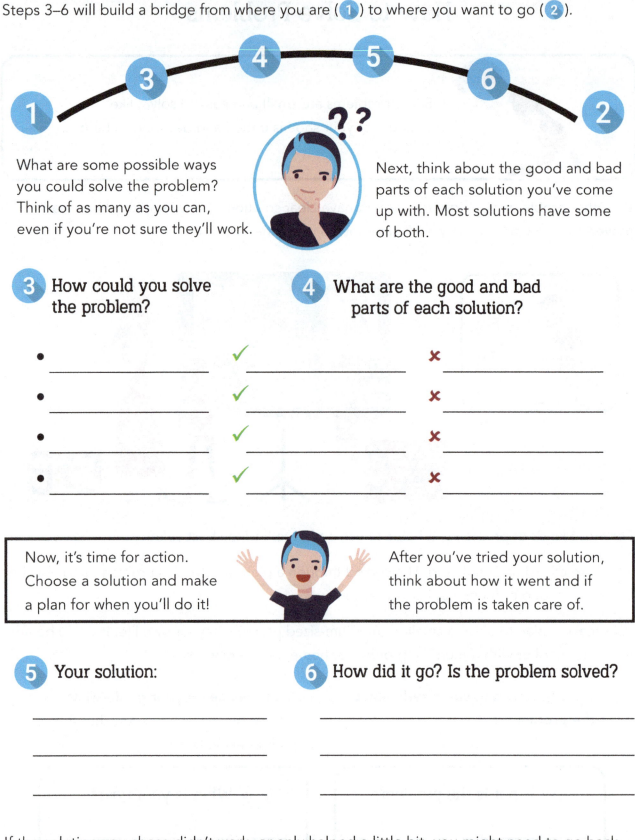

What are some possible ways you could solve the problem? Think of as many as you can, even if you're not sure they'll work.

Next, think about the good and bad parts of each solution you've come up with. Most solutions have some of both.

3 **How could you solve the problem?**

- _____
- _____
- _____
- _____

4 **What are the good and bad parts of each solution?**

✓ _____ ✗ _____
✓ _____ ✗ _____
✓ _____ ✗ _____
✓ _____ ✗ _____

Now, it's time for action. Choose a solution and make a plan for when you'll do it!

After you've tried your solution, think about how it went and if the problem is taken care of.

5 **Your solution:**

_____
_____
_____

6 **How did it go? Is the problem solved?**

_____
_____
_____

If the solution you chose didn't work, or only helped a little bit, you might need to go back to step **3** and repeat the steps from there with a new solution.

With practice, you'll become an expert problem solver!

Practice: How to Solve a Problem

You can use this blank form for working through other problems that come up.

1 What is the problem?

_____

_____

_____

2 What is your goal?

_____

_____

_____

3 How could you solve the problem?

- _____
- _____
- _____
- _____

4 What are the good and bad parts of each solution?

✓ _____ ✗ _____

✓ _____ ✗ _____

✓ _____ ✗ _____

✓ _____ ✗ _____

5 Your solution:

_____

_____

_____

_____

6 How did it go? Is the problem solved?

_____

_____

_____

_____

You can find a blank copy of this form at sethgillihan.com/books/CBT-parents.

Q&A About Mindful CBT

Q: How long will it take before I start to feel better?

A: We can't know exactly how long it will take for you, but mindful CBT can start working quickly, often in 2 to 4 weeks or so.

Q: How can I get the most out of mindful CBT?

A: The more you practice, the sooner you'll start to feel better. It's a good idea to let an adult (probably a parent) know when you need help with any of the skills you're learning.

Q: Will mindful CBT get rid of my difficult feelings?

A: The skills you'll learn in this workbook can help you handle problems and upsetting emotions. They can't make hard things disappear from your life, but they can make it easier to deal with them.

Q: Will I always need to do workbooks like this one?

A: No. Learning mindful CBT is similar *to* learning how to read: After you spend some time learning the new skills, you'll always be able to use them when you need to.

Q: Is mindful CBT the only therapy that works?

A: Definitely not! Many types of therapy have been found to be helpful for kids. The important thing is to find what works for *you*.

Q: Do I need to do every page in this workbook?

A: It's best to do all of part 1, which will teach you the basic skills. When you get to part 2, you can focus on the chapters that apply to you.

Q: My parents want me to do mindful CBT. What's in it for me?

A: Young people often start doing mindful CBT because their parents tell them to, but the aim is to make **your life** better. As you're starting out here, it's good to think about how you would like your own life to improve.

CHAPTER 2

THINK: Retraining Your Brain

In this chapter, we'll explore the CBT skills that focus on the mind and thoughts. You'll learn how to spot the kinds of thoughts that can lead to problems.

Once you know what you're thinking, you'll learn how to find out if a thought is true or not.

You'll also learn about the many tricks the mind can play on us!

As you work through this chapter, you'll build the skills you need to retrain your brain so that your thoughts are more helpful to you.

Let's get started!

What Is Your Mind Up To?

Your mind has a lot to say, and what it says affects how you feel. Let's look at an example.

Sloane's mom is a few minutes late to pick her up. Sloane's mind creates a story to explain why she's late.

It's not surprising that Sloane feels sad and afraid when she believes this story.

Now imagine that her mind instead tells her, "She's just running a little late." How do you think she would feel? You can write your answer in the box below.

She'll probably feel fine, right? You can see how powerful thoughts can be! We can have totally different feelings about the same situation based on what our minds tell us.

Now it's your turn! Fill in the blanks below about a recent time when you felt upset.

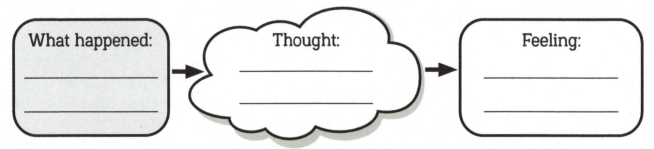

Do your feelings make sense based on the thoughts your mind was telling you?

You'll get lots of practice in this workbook at seeing what your mind is up to!

Are Your Thoughts Always True?

Your mind is amazing. It allows you to do, feel, and think so many things!

But here's the thing about minds: **The stories they tell aren't always true.** So we can wind up feeling upset even though nothing is actually wrong!

That's what happened with Sloane when her mind told her something terrible had happened to her mom. She was very sad and anxious, but a few minutes later, her mom drove up. Nothing bad had happened—she had just gotten stuck in traffic.

Learning to see thoughts as stories that might not be true is one of the most important skills you will ever learn.

But you don't have to question *everything* your mind tells you. That would be exhausting and would use too much brain power!

It's best to take a closer look at what your mind is saying when:

- You suddenly feel very upset
- You keep feeling upset for a long time
- Your actions aren't helping you reach your goals

> ### Question your thoughts but trust yourself!
>
> One time *not* to doubt your thoughts is when you know someone is hurting you in any way or doing something that makes you very uncomfortable.
>
> If this ever happens to you, trust yourself. Tell an adult who can help you, like a parent, teacher, counselor, doctor, or nurse.

With practice, you can learn to think more helpful thoughts. There are three simple steps for helping your mind to think differently. You've already seen the first step: Realize that your mind is telling you a story.

Step 1: Realize

This is a big step. Usually, we just assume our thoughts are true. But some thoughts are **facts**, and some are **stories**.

When Sloane was waiting for her mom, Sloane had some fact thoughts and some story thoughts. Use the following table to decide which of her thoughts are facts (things she *knows*) and which are stories (things she *doesn't know*).

Sloane's Thoughts	Fact	Story
My mom drives a yellow car.		
My mom forgot all about me.		
There must have been a car accident.		
I'm going to be waiting here all night.		
Almost everyone else has been picked up.		

The first and last ones are facts, and the rest are stories. Sloane *knows* the color of her mom's car, but she *doesn't know* if her mom forgot about her.

She also *doesn't know* why her mom was late. Sloane is worried about waiting all night, but that's just a guess her brain made based on her fears.

Now it's your turn.

Think of a recent time when you were feeling upset about something. What was the situation?

_____

_____

What was a **fact** about what happened?

_____

_____

What was a **story** your mind told you about what happened?

_____

_____

Practice: See the Mind's Story

The first step in working with your thoughts is to **Realize** what your mind is telling you. You can use this sheet to practice seeing what your thoughts are up to. The first row is an example.

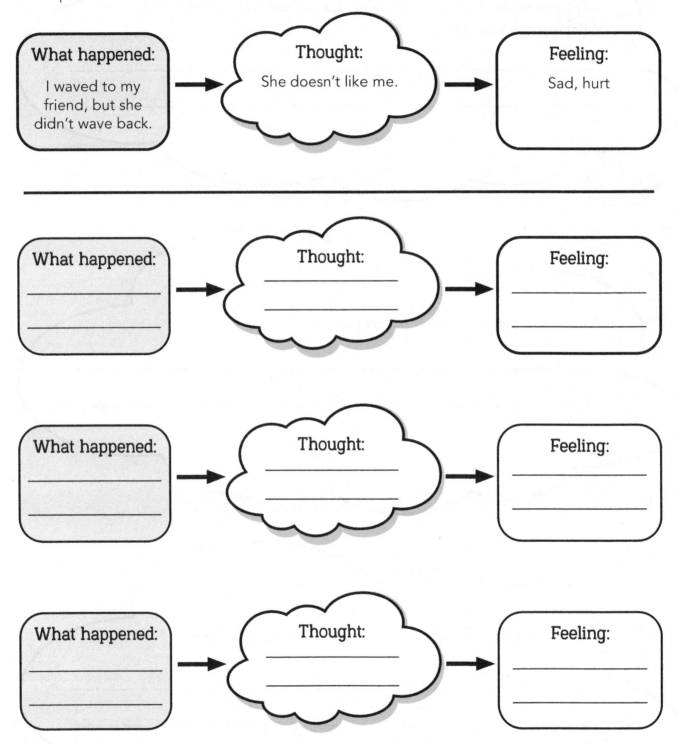

You can find a blank copy of this form at sethgillihan.com/books/CBT-parents.

Discovering If a Thought Is True

Now that you've figured out what you're thinking, you can move on to questioning your thoughts. Some stories are true, like if Sloane had told herself, "My mom is just running late."

You can discover if a thought is true by thinking like a scientist. It's time to do some **research**!

Step 2: Research

Let's take a closer look at the scary story Sloane's mind told her: "Something terrible happened." Scientists look for **evidence**, which tells them what is true and what is not.

As Sloane was waiting for her mom, was there any *good* evidence that something terrible had happened?

_____

_____

In this example, there was no real evidence for this story—it was just a fear, and **fears are not facts**.

Now, what about evidence *against* the story? Again, Sloane didn't know the real reason that her mom was late to pick her up.

"Fears are not facts."

What she did know was that her mind had told her similar stories many times before. But thankfully, they had never been true.

So even though Sloane was feeling very nervous while waiting for her mom, all the **evidence** seemed to say that her mind's scary story was not true. There was no solid reason to believe it.

Let's practice with one of your thoughts. To begin, think of a story your mind told you. You can write it in the space below.

> _____
>
> _____

Great! You've done Step 1: You **realize** what your mind was saying.

Now, it's possible that your thought was exactly right. For example, maybe your mind said, "You're going to be late for school," and you were.

But you'll often find that the mind's stories are not quite right! They ignore some things. They make too big of a deal about other things. They even make things up.

So now we get to put on our scientist hats! Let's do our **research**. Take a moment to look closely at the thought you wrote down. Is it completely true? Let's look at the evidence.

Evidence for the story:	Evidence against the story:
(What tells you this story is true?)	(What says this story might not be true?)
_____	_____
_____	_____
_____	_____
_____	_____
_____	_____
_____	_____

Well done. Now, on to the final step! So far, you've **realized** what the thought was. You've done your **research** to see if it's true. Now it's time to **revise**.

Finding a Better Story

Step 3: Revise

In this step, you get to find a more helpful way of thinking. When Sloane realized her scary thought was just a story, she thought of another way to see things, as you can see in the picture.

This new story helped Sloane to feel less worried and upset. Plus, it turned out to be true!

There are many ways to come up with a better story.

Be your own friend: Think about what you could tell a friend if they were in your shoes.

You made a mistake in a basketball game. → **First thought:** "I'm a terrible player." → **New thought:** "It's okay—everyone makes mistakes."

Think of a better story: The revised thought might not be great, but it's not terrible.

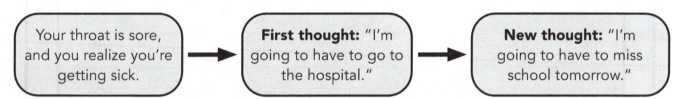

Your throat is sore, and you realize you're getting sick. → **First thought:** "I'm going to have to go to the hospital." → **New thought:** "I'm going to have to miss school tomorrow."

Turn it around: Figure out the opposite of your first thought.

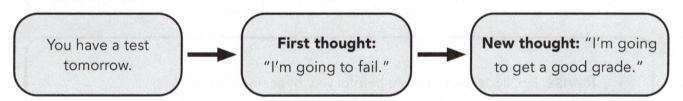

You have a test tomorrow. → **First thought:** "I'm going to fail." → **New thought:** "I'm going to get a good grade."

But what if you don't believe the new thought? It's perfectly okay! What's most important is knowing there are other ways of seeing things. Over time, this practice can help to make the new thoughts more believable.

Now that you've learned the steps, you can practice putting them all together!

Practice: Shift Your Thinking

Use these three steps to see if your mind is telling you something that isn't true.

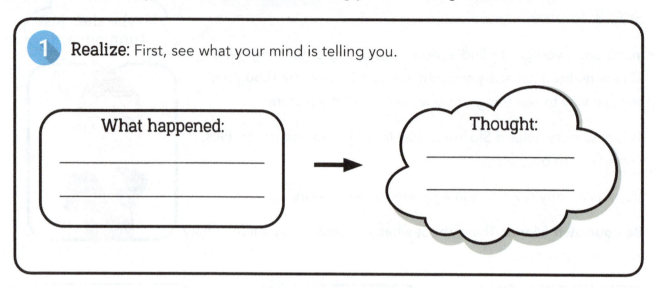

1 **Realize:** First, see what your mind is telling you.

What happened:
_____
_____

→

Thought:
_____
_____

2 **Research:** Next, take a closer look to see if it's true.

What says it is true?	What says it might not be true?
_____	_____
_____	_____
_____	_____

3 **Revise:** Finally, is there a more helpful way of seeing things?

_____
_____
_____
_____

You can find a blank copy of this form at sethgillihan.com/books/CBT-parents.

Learning the Mind's Tricks

When you take a closer look at the mind's stories, you'll start to see some **tricks** it plays on you. These tricks can cause you to believe things that aren't true. They can also affect your feelings and actions in ways that aren't helpful.

You'll often find these mind tricks when you're doing the **Realize-Research-Revise** exercise to see if a mental story is true.

You can think of these different tricks as **mental eyeglasses** that make you see the world in certain ways.

For example, **Fortune-Telling** glasses make it seem like you know what's going to happen in the future, as if you're looking into a crystal ball! But you can't actually know what's going to happen until it does.

Other glasses cause you to **Think with Your Feelings**.

You might feel anxious about going to school, and then you think the anxiety means something bad is going to happen.

But maybe it will turn out to be a great day! So your feelings weren't telling you the truth about how things would go.

Once you know what the mind is up to, you're less likely to fall for its tricks. You can take off those unhelpful glasses and start to see more clearly!

On the next page, you'll find more of the mind's common tricks.

All-or-Nothing Thinking
Seeing things as all good or all bad

Making It Personal
Thinking something is about you when it isn't

Fortune Telling
Thinking you can predict the future

Thinking with Feelings
Treating your feelings as facts

Ignoring the Positive
Telling yourself that good things don't count

Magnifying
Thinking something is much worse than it is

Mind Reading
Believing you know what someone else is thinking

Let's take a closer look at these **mind tricks**. Here are some examples of what our minds can tell us when we're wearing the different mental glasses.

When we're seeing more clearly with those glasses off, we stop believing the false things our minds tell us.

Mind Trick	Glasses On	Glasses Off
All-or-Nothing Thinking	"I'm either good at math or terrible at math."	"I'm good at math even though I don't get perfect grades."
Making It Personal	"My friend is upset, so I must have done something wrong."	"Maybe my friend's feelings aren't about me."
Fortune Telling	"Nobody will want to sit with me at lunch."	"I've always found someone to eat with."
Thinking with Feelings	"Being nervous before my soccer match means I'm going to play badly."	"It's normal to feel anxious before a game or match."
Ignoring the Positive	"She only wants to be my friend because she feels sorry for me."	"She seems to really want to be friends with me."
Magnifying	"I forgot my homework. I'm going to fail."	"I can talk to my teacher about it, and it will be okay."
Mind Reading	"They think my shirt looks dumb."	"They're probably not thinking about me at all!"

CHAPTER 3

ACT:
Doing Things That Make Your Life Better

In this chapter, we'll take a closer look at the kinds of skills that focus on *action*.

As you saw in chapter 1, these skills work really well with the **Think** skills we just went over.

In later chapters, you'll find lots of ways to use the **Act** skills in your life.

Ready to dive in? Let's get started!

How to Make Hard Things Easier

Have you ever tried to do something but found that it was too hard? We've all been there.

That's what happened when Lauren tried to learn a new piece for her string orchestra. She just couldn't seem to learn the notes or the timing.

The more she struggled, the madder she felt toward herself! That night, she told her parents, "I want to quit violin. I'm no good at it."

But when Lauren told her teacher about it, Mrs. Bergstrom knew exactly how to help! First, she guided Lauren in clapping out the rhythm. That way she could learn the timing without needing to think about the notes.

Next, she and Lauren went over the notes one measure at a time. Lauren knew she could learn one measure, so she felt confident that she could learn the whole song. Soon she had learned whole sections of the piece, and her playing was getting smoother and easier.

Mrs. Bergstrom used a practice we use a lot in CBT: She broke something hard into **smaller steps** to make it easier.

When a task is too *hard*, it usually means it's too *big*! It's like trying to change a lightbulb in the ceiling while standing on the floor. You don't need to "work harder" to reach the ceiling . . . you just need a ladder! A ladder turns a really big gap (from the floor to the lightbulb) into a bunch of little gaps that are easy to climb one by one.

The same goes for any task you're trying to complete. The whole thing might feel like too much. Maybe you're not sure how to do it, or even where to start. **But if you break the task into smaller pieces, each one will feel like something you can do.**

You can use the same skill when you're feeling so overwhelmed by a big activity that you don't even want to begin.

Here are some big activities that can feel like too much all at once:

Writing a paper or report for school

Learning a new topic in school

Getting ready in the morning

Completing a hard puzzle

Finishing your homework

Reading a whole book

Getting ready for bed

Cleaning your room

Setting the table

Running a mile

Doing chores

But imagine chopping that too-big chore into tiny steps that are easy to do. That way, it will be easier to get started and to keep going. **Just focus on doing one small step at a time**, and before you know it, you'll be done!

Now it's your turn. What is a big job you need to do?

My big job:

Next, what are three smaller chunks you can break it into?

Do you need to divide any of those three steps into even smaller steps? If so, you can write them in the boxes below.

On the next page, you'll find a blank practice form for breaking down tasks. Have fun making hard jobs easier!

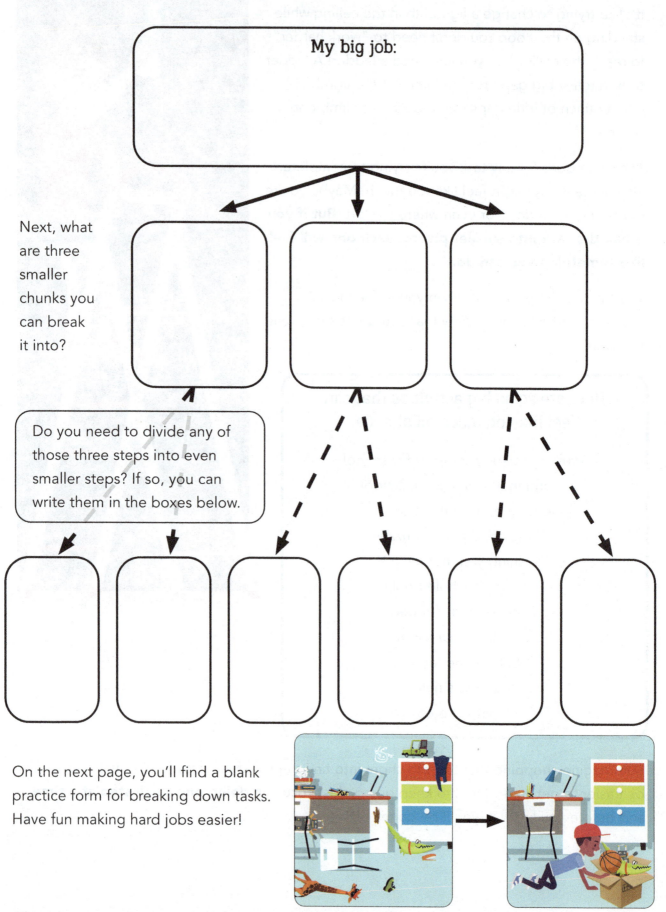

Practice: Break It Down

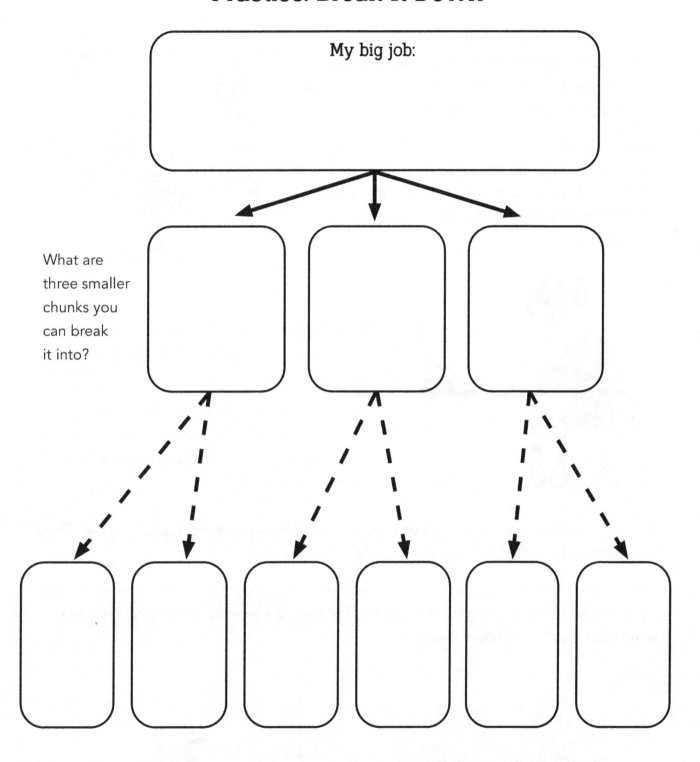

My big job:

What are three smaller chunks you can break it into?

Use the additional boxes above if you need to break your tasks into even smaller pieces.

You can find a blank copy of this form at sethgillihan.com/books/CBT-parents.

How to Do More Activities That Boost Your Mood

When a person is feeling sad or down, there are two kinds of activities that can lead to happiness and make people feel better about their lives: things that are fun and things that are important.

Fun activities are things you enjoy doing. Different people enjoy different things, but the activities often include playing, relaxing, or spending time with friends. You feel good while you're doing something fun.

Important activities are ones you might not *like* doing, but you *need* to do them so things will go well in your life.

Important activities often involve some kind of work, such as doing your homework. And unlike fun activities, the good feelings they give you usually come later.

You might not love doing these activities, but you feel happy about completing them. There is something satisfying about taking care of what's important.

For example, Ada and Faye love to play with their guinea pigs; that's a fun activity for them. On the other hand, cleaning out the guinea pigs' cage is important but not fun; they feel good after they've finished this job.

Now it's your turn! What is an activity that's fun for you? You can write it or draw a picture of it in the box below.

```
My fun activity:



```

How about something that's important?

```
My important activity:



```

You probably know already that some activities are both fun *and* important. Just because you have to do something doesn't mean you don't also *like* to do it!

Maybe you love going to school, or you have fun while you're exercising. It's a great bonus when one activity does both things for you!

On the other hand, some things you do might not be fun *or* important. For example, lying on the couch might just feel boring, and it's not something that's important to do.

It's best not to spend too much time doing these kinds of things. Otherwise, your days will feel pretty empty.

Building Good Things Into Your Life

The first step is to see what's filling your days right now. Taking a look at what you're already doing will help you see what kinds of activities you'll want to do more often.

All you'll need to do for this part is **keep track of what you did each day**. You'll also rate how fun and important each activity was. That way, you'll know if you need to do more fun things, more important things, or some of both.

Here's an example from part of my day so far to give you an idea of what this looks like.

Time	Activity	Fun (0–10)	Important (0–10)
8–9 a.m.	Taking Faye to school	6	10
9–10 a.m.	Designing this workbook	8	9
10–11 a.m.			
11 a.m.–12 p.m.	Working in the garden	10	7
12–1 p.m.	Lunch	7	9

Your activities probably won't fit neatly into the one-hour blocks on the form, and that's fine. For example, taking Faye to school took only about 30 minutes, and making and eating my lunch took closer to 45 minutes.

Just fill in the form as best you can. And remember—it does not have to be "perfect"!

On the next page, you'll find a blank form for keeping track of your activities. It's best to fill it out as you go through your day. You can also do it at the end of each day. The sooner you record your activities, the easier it is to remember what you did and what it was like for you.

Practice: Track Your Activities

Time	Activity	Fun (0–10)	Important (0–10)
6–7 a.m.			
7–8 a.m.			
8–9 a.m.			
9–10 a.m.			
10–11 a.m.			
11 a.m.–12 p.m.			
12–1 p.m.			
1–2 p.m.			
2–3 p.m.			
3–4 p.m.			
4–5 p.m.			
5–6 p.m.			
6–7 p.m.			
7–8 p.m.			
8–9 p.m.			
9–10 p.m.			

You can find a blank copy of this form at sethgillihan.com/books/CBT-parents.

I suggest filling out these forms for at least 3 or 4 days, so you have a good idea of how you're spending your time. (You can find blank forms at the web address on the bottom of the form.)

While you're tracking your activities, you can keep going with the next steps. You're going to come up with lists of fun activities and important ones. With that in mind, we've created lists of activities on the next page that can help you get started.

Keep in mind that what's fun or important is up to *you*! Just because something is on my lists doesn't mean you have to put it on yours. And, of course, feel free to add things to your lists that aren't on mine.

One final pro tip: Aim to make *most* of your activities screen-free—not on a phone, tablet, or other device. Research shows that there are many good things about enjoying nature, playing with friends, moving your body, and doing other activities that aren't screen-based.

I want you to get the most out of the things you'll be doing, and that means discovering all that life has to offer!

After looking at the example list, you'll create your own list of activities. You'll also decide if completing each activity will be easy, medium, or hard for you. These ratings will help you choose the easier ones to do first. Over time, you'll work up to the harder ones.

Important activities:

Feeding my pet

Going to school

Doing homework

Making my bed

Brushing my teeth

Cleaning my room

Watering my plant

Weeding the garden

Doing schoolwork

Clearing the table

Going to the doctor

Taking out the trash

Taking a bath or shower

Putting away my clothes

Going to sports practice

Unloading the dishwasher

Writing a thank-you card

Getting dressed for the day

Practicing a musical instrument

Fun activities:

Doing puzzles

Writing a story

Playing outside

Visiting the zoo

Going to a movie

Watching television

Throwing a frisbee

Going to a concert

Having a friend over

Playing video games

Going for a bike ride

Playing a board game

Petting my dog or cat

Having fun with family

Playing with my sibling

Dressing up in costumes

Reading a favorite book

Going to the playground

Visiting a children's museum

Practice: Activity Lists

Fun		Important	
Activity	Easy/Med/Hard	Activity	Easy/Med/Hard

Creating Your Short List of Activities

Now that you've got your lists, let's pick the activities you'll be starting with. This step will help you focus your efforts on a small number of activities.

In this step, you're going to pick the top 10 activities that you'll be doing first. I suggest choosing ones that will **have the most value to you**. That could mean they're ones you're most excited to do. Or they could be things that are a bit urgent, such as needing to catch up on homework.

You can choose a balance of fun and important activities—about five of each—or more of one or the other. You'll decide how many of each to include based on what you need in your life.

In the right-hand column, you can write "I" for important activities and "F" for fun ones.

Activity	Important (I) or Fun (F)

Now you're ready for the final step! You're going to choose things to do, and when you'll do them.

Putting the activities into your schedule is really important. It's much easier to do something if we have a specific time when we're planning to do it. That way, it's easier to remember what you want to do, and other things won't get in the way.

Take a look at your short list of activities. What is the first thing you'd like to do? It's best to **start with something easy**. You can write it in the box on the right.

Great! Now let's choose a day and time. You may need to talk with your parents for this step, especially if you'll need their help with the activity, like if you want to invite a friend to come over.

When would be a good time to plan to do this activity? You can circle the day and write in the time.

Finally, will you need to do anything to prepare for this activity? For example, if you're planning to ride your bike, you might need to pump up the tires and find your helmet. You can write down any prep work you'll need to do.

Now you're all set to do your first planned activity! I wish you all the best as you do it, and I hope you get a lot out of it.

First activity:

_____

Sun   Mon   Tue   Wed   Thu   Fri   Sat

Time:

_____

How to prepare:

_____

_____

_____

_____

Nice Work!

After you complete your first activity, you can keep going! Keep working through your short list of activities, starting with the easier ones. When you're ready, you can move on to the activities that are a bit harder.

When you run out of activities to do, you can add another ten from your big lists of fun and important things. You can always repeat things you've already done, too.

Common Questions

What if I forgot to do my activity?

No problem—it's easy to forget. Next time, just set an alarm or write a note to remind yourself.

What if it felt too hard to do?

That happens a lot. You can use the skill of breaking things down to make it easier to get started!

What if I do my activity but don't feel better?

Sometimes the activity leads to good feelings right away. But often, it takes a while before you feel any different. It's like with exercise—you won't be faster after running one time, but you will with continued practice.

How long will I need to do this?

It's a good idea to stick with this program for at least a month. After that point, you can shift toward letting these activities just become a part of your everyday life!

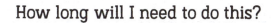

43

How to Overcome Things That Scare You

Everyone has things they're afraid of. Some of these fears are useful. It's helpful when you feel afraid of something that is actually dangerous!

A fear of moving cars, for example, helps us to look both ways before we cross the street. A fear of what might happen if we swim alone helps us to stay safe in the water.

But another kind of fear isn't helpful. Being afraid of the dark while in a safe bed isn't helpful and makes it hard to go to sleep. A fear of harmless dogs can get in the way of going over to friends' houses or playing in parks.

But I have good news for you! There is a simple way to get past your fear of things that won't actually hurt you.

The most helpful way to reduce unhelpful fear is to face it.

That's right! If you do the thing that you're afraid to do, it becomes less scary.

The best way to overcome a fear of dogs is to start spending time with nice dogs.

The best way to overcome a fear of the dark is to spend more time alone in the dark.

The best way to overcome a fear of talking to people is to talk to people again and again.

When you face something you're afraid of, your fear will get smaller. There are thousands of research studies showing that this is true.

What's more, I myself have experienced this way to shrink fear. And not just as a therapist helping other people with their fears. I used this skill to finally get over my fear of the dark . . . when I was nearly 30 years old!

To see why it's so helpful to face your fears, let's go back to the **CBT Triangle**.

Remember Drew? She was very afraid of dogs.

It's easy to see why she wanted to avoid dogs. She felt afraid of them and thought they would hurt her.

But avoiding dogs actually made her fear worse!

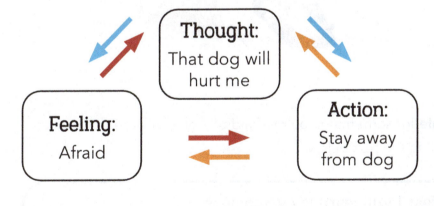

Each time she stays away from a dog, her brain believes the dog must be dangerous.

It's as if her brain is thinking, "Drew is avoiding that dog— it must be dangerous! Good thing she stayed away."

If Drew went up to the dog, her brain would learn something new: *It's not going to hurt me.* But when she avoids it, her brain doesn't get that new information.

Drew also feels a little bit of relief when she avoids a dog, which feels better than being afraid. Because of this feeling of relief, her brain learns that it must be better to avoid dogs.

The more we avoid what we fear, the scarier it will seem. **The more we face our fears, the more they will shrink.**

Now it's your turn.

Let's make your own **CBT Triangle** for something you're afraid of. You can write down what the fear is (or draw a picture of it) in the box below.

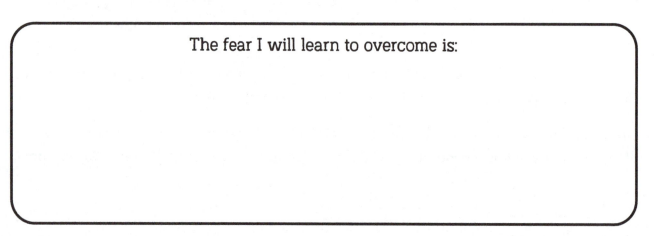

The fear I will learn to overcome is:

Fill in your CBT Triangle about this fear:

- What scary **thought** do you have about it?

- What **feeling** have you noticed?

- How have you been avoiding (**action**) the thing you fear?

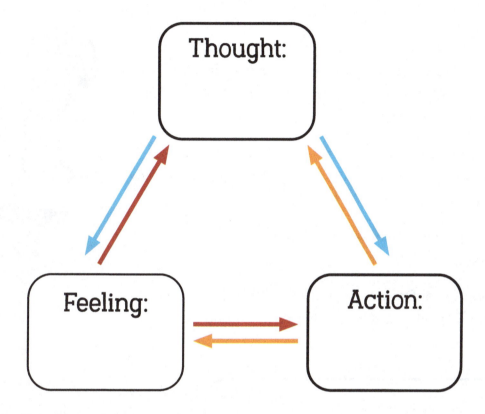

When you replace avoiding your fear with facing your fear, your fear will get smaller.

Your thoughts will change, too. For example, when Drew started spending time with dogs, she realized, "They're actually cute and sweet."

How do you think your own thoughts might change because you're facing what you're afraid of?

New thought:

_____

_____

_____

_____

At this point, you might be thinking, "It sounds great to be less afraid. But how do I face something that's so scary?" It can feel like a terrifying thing to do!

Here's the secret: **We'll do it little by little, not all at once.**

You've already learned how this works with doing a big job. Breaking it down makes it much easier.

It's the same with facing your fears. The idea of a ladder fits perfectly here. The way to conquer a big fear is to break it into a series of steps. Each step builds on the ones before, just like climbing the rungs of a ladder.

Let's see how this process worked for Drew. First, she made a **courage ladder.** Her courage ladder started at the bottom with easier ways to face her fear.

The lowest steps have lower ratings, which can go from 1 (easiest) to 10 (hardest).

The first step was for Drew to be around a little dog who was on a leash (rated a 1), and the scariest thing was petting a big dog (rated a 9).

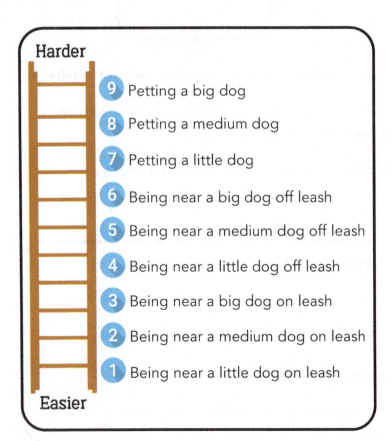

Harder

9 Petting a big dog

8 Petting a medium dog

7 Petting a little dog

6 Being near a big dog off leash

5 Being near a medium dog off leash

4 Being near a little dog off leash

3 Being near a big dog on leash

2 Being near a medium dog on leash

1 Being near a little dog on leash

Easier

Each step was a little more challenging than the one before, just like how each rung of a ladder is a little higher than the one below it.

When Drew first walked up to the little dog, she felt very scared.

But when she stayed near the dog, she got used to it pretty quickly, and her fear got smaller.

Once she felt more comfortable with this first step, it wasn't that much harder for Drew to hang out with a medium-sized dog on a leash (rated a 2).

Soon Drew was able to work up to being around a medium-sized dog off a leash (a 5), because she had already gotten comfortable with the earlier steps! You see how this works?

What Is Courage?

It might seem like courage is the *opposite* of fear.

But courage is not a feeling. **It's deciding to do something even though it feels scary.**

So when you feel afraid to take a courage step, that's exactly what makes it courage!

You don't have to make the fear go away. Let it be there as you boldly take your courage step.

Now it's your turn.

You can make your own courage ladder. Just think of ways you can face your fear.

Come up with a list that includes easier steps, some harder ones, and some steps that are in the middle.

It works best if the steps are gradual, instead of having some that are really easy and some that are really hard.

That would be like a ladder with only bottom and top rungs! You'll want to fill in the spaces in between so it's easier to climb.

You can write your steps and their ratings in the table on the next page. As a reminder, a 1 would be very easy to do, and a 10 would be really difficult.

49

Practice: Make a Courage Ladder

Activity	Rating (1–10)

You can find a blank copy of this form at sethgillihan.com/books/CBT-parents.

How to Face Fears

Once you've made your courage ladder, you're ready to start climbing! Here are a few things to keep in mind as you do.

Plan: First, it usually works best to **plan a specific time** to take a courage step. That way, you can prepare for it, and it's less likely that something else will get in the way.

Part of planning might include talking with a parent or other adult about any help you may need. For example, if you'll need a ride, you can plan with your mom or dad for a time that works.

Stay: As you take a courage step, aim to **stay in the frightening situation long enough that your brain learns something new.**

It's like getting used to cold water in a swimming pool. If you dipped your foot in the pool for a couple seconds, your body wouldn't have a chance to get more comfortable in the water.

And you might have even more dread of the water after feeling how cold it was!

But if you got all the way into the pool and played for a few minutes, the water would stop feeling so cold.

Soon you would just be focused on how much fun you were having!

It's the same with facing each fear. **Plan to stay a while.** A good sign that you've stayed long enough is when you notice you don't feel as afraid.

Staying around 15 to 30 minutes is usually a good idea.

What to Do After Completing a Courage Step

The first thing to do after finishing a step is to **congratulate yourself**. Any step you take is a big step. Well done!

I'm always proud of people I work with for facing their fear. I hope you can take some pride in your actions, too.

There are a few directions you can go next. First, you could **pause and take a well-earned break**. Rest, relax, and do something nice for yourself.

You might choose instead to **keep going**. Maybe you're excited to take another step, so it feels right to move on up your ladder.

You may be especially eager to continue if the step you took turned out to be easier than you expected.

Whenever you decide to stop, you'll have a couple options for when you start again.

You might choose to **move up to a new step**. Or you might need to **repeat the last step you did**.

It's very normal to repeat a step. It takes time for the brain to learn to feel less afraid. Sometimes it will need more practice.

You don't have to rush up your courage ladder. Take the time you need.

What's more important than your fear?

Why would anyone choose to face what scares them?

Because something is more important to them than their fear.

For Drew, it was wanting to stay with her friends even when dogs were around. She was tired of turning down invitations from friends who had dogs at home.

Think about what's more important to you than your own fear. **What makes you willing to practice courage?**

You can write down or draw whatever comes to mind in the space below.

When you're working up your courage ladder, remind yourself why it's worth it! Remember what you value more than your fear.

When Am I Done?

It's best to climb all the way to the top of your courage ladder—again, as slowly or as quickly as you're able to. That way, your fear will shrink as small as possible.

You'll also have more freedom to do the things you want to do when you've faced everything on your list.

For example, Drew kept going up her courage ladder after getting more comfortable being around small dogs on leashes. She worked up to being able to pet a big dog.

Now Drew can go over to friends' houses even if they have big dogs! She can even pet them if she wants to.

Drew still feels a little nervous around some dogs, but her fear is manageable and doesn't control her actions.

The best part for Drew is that she doesn't have to worry anymore about whether there will be a dog at her friend's house or how big the dog will be. She can just think about how fun it will be to play with her friend!

So once you start climbing, keep coming back to your courage steps. I am confident that you can reach the top!

Once you've taken all your courage steps and aren't feeling much fear anymore, you probably won't have to do these exercises all the time. Courage steps will just be a part of your life.

For Drew, that meant being around dogs more often. She didn't need to plan specific ways and times to face her fear. Being around dogs was built into her days because she was no longer trying to avoid them.

One more thing to keep in mind: **Fear can come back if we start avoiding things again.** If you notice that you're staying away from certain steps on your courage ladder, it's a great idea to face those things on purpose. It is easier to shrink a fear when it's still small, rather than waiting until it gets really big.

In life, we're either moving toward courage or moving toward fear. So just remember:

Avoiding what you fear makes fear grow.

Facing what you fear makes fear shrink.

"We're either moving toward courage or moving toward fear."

How to Work Through Disagreements

There are so many ways we can disagree with another person!

A friend says something that hurts your feelings.

Your parents seem to be treating you unfairly.

A sibling uses your things without asking.

A cousin won't let you have your turn playing video games.

Think of a time in the past few days when you've had a conflict. You can write it or draw it below.

We'll be working through this example in the pages ahead.

There are different ways to handle a conflict. Some of them work better than others! Let's take a closer look at what works, what doesn't, and why.

Being Passive

Kobe and his cousin Jayson both want to play Kobe's new video game.

One way to handle this conflict is to be **passive**.

When we're passive, we give all the power to the other person. They win, we lose.

We think about what *they* want and ignore or hide what *we* want.

In the scene to the right, Kobe is being passive.

Jayson winds up playing the game the whole time he is over at Kobe's house, and Kobe never gets a turn.

Kobe feels mad and hurt about what happened because it doesn't seem fair, but he swallows those feelings and doesn't let Jayson know.

Now it's your turn. What would a **passive** response look like in your own situation? You can describe it or draw it below.

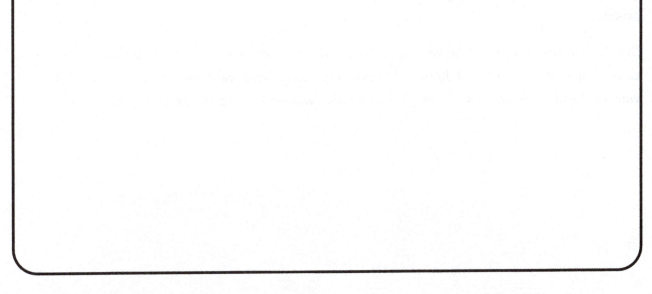

Being Aggressive

The opposite of passive is **aggressive**. Instead of making the other person happy, we focus on our own happiness. We want to *win* and the other person to *lose*.

When we're aggressive, we ignore the other person's feelings and wishes. We only care about getting what we want.

Here's what Kobe did when he was being aggressive.

Jayson isn't very happy about how Kobe is acting. It seems like all Kobe cares about is getting his way. After this argument, Jayson doesn't feel excited to go over to Kobe's house again.

But Jayson isn't the only one who feels bad. Later on, when Kobe is feeling calmer, he doesn't like how he treated Jayson. He likes his cousin and wants him to be happy. Kobe wanted to play his new video game, but he also wishes he had let Jayson have a turn.

Now it's your turn. What would it look like if you tried an **aggressive** solution in your own situation?

So far, neither of these approaches works very well. Being passive doesn't look out for your own needs, and it gives all the power to the other person.

Being aggressive doesn't leave room for the other person's needs, and it tries to keep all the power for yourself.

There's one more approach that usually doesn't work so well. It's a blend of passive and aggressive called . . . **passive-aggressive**. (Surprise!)

Passive-aggressive is not a nice balance somewhere in the middle. It's more like combining the worst parts of passive *and* aggressive!

Being Passive-Aggressive

With this blended approach, you don't try to get what you want. But you also don't give the other person what they want. So you both lose.

For example, Kobe might tell Jayson he can play the video game. But then, instead of letting his friend enjoy the game, Kobe keeps walking in front of the screen and making sounds he knows will annoy Jayson.

When Jayson asks Kobe how to do a special move with his player, Kobe tells him the wrong buttons to press. Kobe is actually being aggressive, but in a way that's more passive.

Jayson winds up getting frustrated and quits the game, so Kobe starts playing it.

You can probably see that a passive-aggressive approach is bad for relationships! It's a dishonest way of pretending to give the other person what they want while actually trying to make them unhappy.

As you think about your own situation, can you imagine a **passive-aggressive** way to handle it? You can write or draw it in the box below.

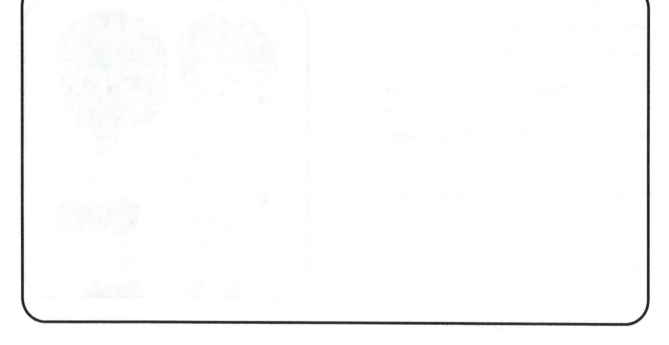

Being Assertive

Now we come to the fourth and final way: to be **assertive**. This is a win-win approach.

When we're assertive, we think about our own rights *and* the other person's.

We aim to find a way that *both* of us can end up happy.

We are honest and direct about what we want and how we feel.

60

You're willing to **share** power, so you and the other person both have a say in finding a solution.

You take seriously what the other person wants **as well as** your own needs and wishes.

When Kobe chose to be assertive, he thought about what he wanted and *also* what Jayson wanted. Here's what he came up with.

Kobe knows Jayson is eager to play. But it doesn't seem right to him to let Jayson go first when Kobe hasn't even played his own game yet.

So Kobe finds a way to suggest what feels okay to him, while also letting Jayson know that his feelings count, too.

You see how that's different from being passive, aggressive, or passive-aggressive? Someone loses in each of those approaches. **But being assertive means that everyone can win!**

Kobe feels good about getting to play first. And Jayson is pleased that Kobe thought about him and that his cousin is going to let him play.

You can also see how being assertive means **you're willing to work together**, because the power is being shared. Kobe presents an idea as a possible solution. He doesn't say, "This is what we're doing, and too bad if you don't like it!"

It's more like: "Look, I like you. You like me. Let's find a way that works for both of us."

Let's go back to your own situation once more. Now that we've worked through four different ways of handling a conflict, think of an **assertive** response to the other person.

Decide what you might say to them. You can also think about what your tone of voice would be like. How could you find a solution that's a win-win?

Great job working through this conflict to find an assertive solution! There will be many times when you don't agree with someone, so you'll have lots of chances to practice being assertive.

CHAPTER 4

BE:
Living Right Here, Right Now

Ready to learn more about mindfulness? That's what this chapter is all about.

Mindfulness is a very powerful practice that's based on a super simple idea, as you saw in chapter 1.

We'll take a closer look at what it means to be mindful and at the ways in which mindfulness can be helpful.

We'll also do some simple exercises that will help introduce you to mindfulness.

If you're ready to get started, there's no time like the present!

The Power of Being Right Where You Are

Did you know that a lot of the time you're not where you are? I mean, your *body* is always right here. But often, your mind is in some other place!

Maybe you're brushing your teeth but thinking about a test you have tomorrow. Your body is in the bathroom, but your mind is in your classroom.

Or you're sitting in class, but your mind has jumped ahead to the doctor's appointment you have later that day.

It's great to be able to think about things that aren't happening right now. You can plan for the future or remember the past.

But sometimes the mind likes to find things to worry about. Or it keeps thinking about something embarrassing that happened, making you cringe again and again!

A whole lot of the time, what upsets us isn't what's going on right now, but something from the past or in the future. That's a big part of why mindfulness can be so helpful.

When you're mindful, you notice what's happening right now.

Letting Go of Worries

When you bring your attention into the present, you're not caught up in worries about things that might happen.

You're just doing what you're doing, right where you are.

Even if there's a problem right now, it helps to be in the present. That way, you're taking care of the problem and not worrying about all the unknowns ahead.

Moving On from Mistakes

It doesn't feel good to mess up in some way. But the mind often holds on to the mistake, so you keep feeling bad about it.

But mistakes we've made are always **in the past**! With mindful attention, we can gently bring our mind **into the present**.

Instead of seeing mistakes as something bad about you, you can realize they're a chance to learn and grow.

And you can move on from mistakes and disappointments, so the past doesn't hold you back.

You Can Feel Calm in Tough Times

As you saw in chapter 1, mindfulness is great for when you're **dealing with difficult feelings**. You'll be learning more ways to plug into that sense of calm throughout this book.

"Storms" in life

Calm below

You Can Enjoy What You're Doing

Mindfulness isn't just about dealing with hard things. It can also make the good things better! When you're mindful, you **notice what's happening right now**.

When you're riding your bike, you can feel the wind on your face and the sunshine on your skin.

If you're swimming, you can sense the cool water all around you and the feeling of your body floating.

When you're with friends, you can really be with them—right there, having fun together.

I imagine you're already being fully present in a lot of these activities. It just feels like having fun and enjoying your life!

You Can Be Nicer to Yourself

Last but not least, mindfulness helps you **treat yourself as a friend**. Being mindful includes accepting yourself as you are.

You can learn to go easy on yourself, even when you've made a mistake.

And you can look out for yourself, knowing you're someone worth taking care of.

It's easy to see that being mindful—being aware of what's happening right here, right now—can lead to many good things. But *how* can you "be mindful?"

Let's take a closer look at how to be in the present and connect with that calmer place inside you.

Practicing Being with Your Breath

As simple as mindfulness is, it takes practice to be in the here and now.

You already saw one way to practice in chapter 1. We took some calming breaths to help you connect with that peaceful place inside you.

That simple approach is one of the most common ways to practice being present. You've probably heard of it—it's called **meditation**.

When you meditate, you just let your mind find a little stillness. You give it a rest from all the thinking and planning and working that it's good at doing.

You give your mind a break by allowing your attention to focus on something that's constant and steady. There are lots of things you can focus on, but the most common one is your breath. Here's how it works.

You can start by sitting comfortably. Close your eyes if you want, or you can keep them open. Take a couple moments to settle in.

1 Start by **focusing** on your breathing. Feel the air coming in as you inhale and going out as you exhale. You might notice your belly getting bigger when you breathe in and smaller when you breathe out.

You can picture your belly as a balloon. It fills up when air comes into your lungs, and it shrinks when you breathe the air out.

2 It won't be long before your mind **drifts**. Soon you'll be thinking about something besides your breath—school, your friends, your parents, or anything at all. It's no problem when the mind wanders to other things. It's what minds like to do!

3 At some point, you'll realize your mind has wandered. You might realize it right away, or it could take a long time. Either way is fine!

Whenever you notice you've lost your focus, just gently **return** your attention back to your breath. You don't need to criticize yourself for thinking about other things or be upset with your mind for wandering.

You can simply come back to the beginning: start once more with step 1. That cycle—**focus**, **drift**, and **return**—is what it means to meditate!

Let yourself relax into this process. It's not anything you have to make a big deal about, and it's not some super serious exercise. It's just breathing! You're simply spending a little time with your breath.

Some people like to set a timer for a few minutes when they're meditating. If you do, you can start with short sessions, maybe 1 to 3 minutes.

Or you can just do a few rounds of breath without a timer. It's *your* meditation, so it's up to you! Even a few focused breaths can be really helpful to your body and brain.

Having as Much Enjoyment as You Can

Mindfulness isn't only for meditation! No matter when you're doing, you can be present while you do it.

Be Curious

One way to enjoy your life more is to **explore** it, like it's the first time you've ever been on this planet!

Imagine you're a visitor from Mars and this is your first time on Earth. What do you notice is happening around you? Who or what do you see?

Use Your Senses

Your senses will help you to take in what's going on around you. Try out this 5 – 4 – 3 – 2 – 1 exercise right now to practice. (But of course, only taste things that are safe to eat! You can also just notice any taste in your mouth.)

5 – 4 – 3 – 2 – 1

5 Things I see:

_____

_____

_____

_____

_____

4 Things I hear:

_____

_____

_____

3 Things I feel:

_____

_____

_____

2 Things I smell:

_____

_____

1 Thing I taste:

_____

Take Your Time

Do you ever find yourself *rushing* to get to the next thing? It might feel like what you're doing is taking too long, and you just want to get it done as fast as you can.

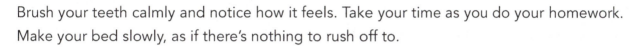

But that's not a very fun way to be all the time. It's not relaxing, and it makes it harder to do a good job.

See what it's like instead to **let something take as long as it takes**.

Brush your teeth calmly and notice how it feels. Take your time as you do your homework. Make your bed slowly, as if there's nothing to rush off to.

Sometimes you'll need to go quickly, like when a parent asks you to hurry so you won't be late.

But when you're able to, try dropping the rush and ease into what you're doing.

What are some activities where you can practice taking your time?

Take-My-Time Activities:

- _____
- _____
- _____
- _____
- _____
- _____

Let Life Be an Adventure

Life is a bit like a video game. There are always new problems to solve and challenges to face. Without these problems, video games and life would be pretty boring!

When a problem comes up, **treat it like you're playing a game**. Imagine you need to solve it to move to the "next level"!

Let difficult things become moments for trying out your skills and building new strengths.

Welcoming the Unknown

It can be scary not knowing what's going to happen. You might worry that things won't go the way you want them to, or that there will be some bad surprise.

For example, maybe you're worried about how your test is going to go, or if you're going to make friends at your new school.

It's normal to feel anxious about the unknown. What is one unknown that's been on your mind lately?

But there's another way of greeting this uncertainty. See what it's like to **welcome the mystery of what's ahead**. You have a whole adventure that's coming, and *no one* knows exactly what will happen. Some of the surprises that are coming might even be really good things!

Rather than making the unknown a problem, **open up to it**. How does it feel to bring your spirit of adventure to the unknown future?

An Unknown in My Life:

_____

_____

_____

Watching What's Happening Inside You

What if I throw up at school?

Sometimes the things that happen inside of you can feel upsetting.

Upsetting thoughts can make you feel anxious, angry, or sad.

Strong feelings can be uncomfortable.

Body sensations might feel like there's an alarm going off inside your body, or like your stomach is tied in knots.

It's normal to try to get rid of these things. We would rather make the difficult thoughts, feelings, or sensations go away.

But here's an experiment for you to try: Don't think about an elephant for the next 30 seconds. Ready? Begin!

(30 seconds later) I can guess what happened. You probably thought about an elephant . . . a lot! That's what happens when we try to push things away. They keep coming back, stronger than ever!

Our minds have to keep watching out for whatever we're trying to get rid of. Your mind was saying, "Am I thinking of an elephant? What about now? Any elephants?" Trying to make thoughts, feelings, or sensations go away makes it more likely that we'll have exactly those experiences!

There's a more helpful way to deal with these difficult things. Become the **Observer**. Just watch these experiences, without trying to make them stop.

As the Observer, you can just notice your thoughts. They're just things the mind says, which a lot of the time aren't even true!

You can breathe with feelings. Allow yourself to feel what you feel.

And you can feel the sensations in your body, with curiosity, like a map maker studying a location.

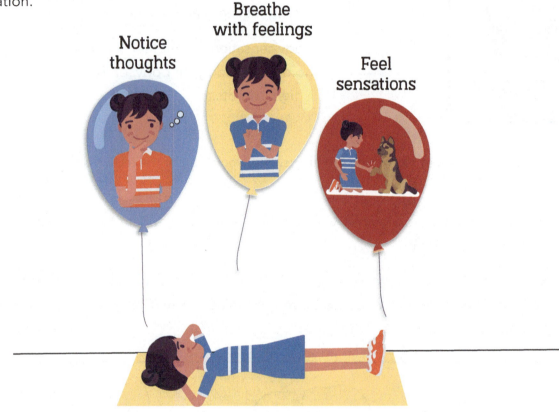

When you're the Observer, you become like a mountain. A mountain is strong and steady. Even when there are winds and storms and rain, the mountain is solid and unmoved.

A deep and steady strength lives inside you, too. You can observe all the "storms" in your life from that place as you practice being the Observer.

Part 2
USING THE SKILLS

The rest of this workbook shows you how to use the skills you've learned to deal with many difficult things. Pages with blue headings are **Think** skills. Pages with orange headings are **Act** skills. Pages with purple headings are **Be** skills.

The topics in this half of the workbook are divided into four sections:

I. Taming Anxiety
Chapters 5–11

II. Working Through Challenging Emotions
Chapters 12–15

III. Getting Things Done
Chapters 16–19

IV. Managing Relationships
Chapters 20–21

I. Taming Anxiety

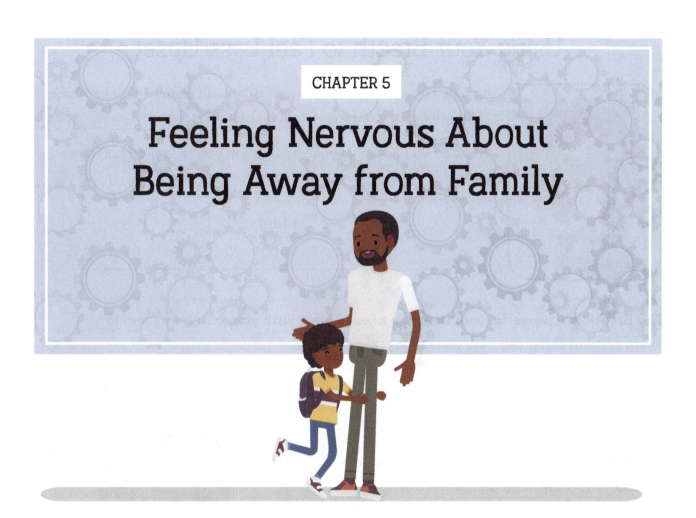

CHAPTER 5

Feeling Nervous About Being Away from Family

A lot of young people feel anxious about being away from home or from their parents. Familiar people and places feel safe, and separation can be scary.

Sometimes the worry is that something bad will happen to you, such as getting hurt while you and your parents are apart. Or it could be about not having your parents there to comfort you if you feel upset.

Other times, the worry is about what might happen to your family. Or maybe you just like it better when you're at home with your family, and you're not sure what's upsetting about being separated.

In this chapter, you'll discover how your thoughts, actions, and attention can make it easier to spend time apart.

Using Your Breath to Feel Less Upset

Anxiety turns on an alarm in your brain and body. That alarm says, "Something is wrong! Watch out! Look for danger!"

What do you notice in your body when you're feeling nervous about being away from your family?

I feel:

_____

The breath is a powerful tool that you *always* have with you. It's closely tied to your alarm system, and it can help you to feel calmer.

Here's what to do:

1 Breathe in through your nose while you count to 2. Let the breaths be gentle and easy.

2 Breathe slowly out your nose while you count to 4. Slow breaths turn down the danger alarm.

3 Continue these breaths for a minute or longer—in for 2, out for 4.

4 Finally, notice what your senses are telling you. What do you see, hear, feel, smell, or taste?

These slow breaths are a nice way to prepare for the other skills that help with anxiety.

Treating Yourself Like a Friend

We usually think of a friend as someone besides ourselves. But you can also be your *own* friend!

This might sound surprising at first, but **you have a relationship with yourself**.

Think of the ways you already relate to yourself—talking to yourself, reminding yourself not to forget something, sometimes calling yourself mean names.

This relationship with yourself can be an amazing source of comfort when you're away from home and family. You can never be separated from yourself, so you have a friend wherever you go!

What does it mean to treat yourself like a friend? It might help to think about how you would want a friend to treat you.

You can jot down some ideas in the box below. I've listed a few to help you get started.

How to be my own friend:

Remind myself that I'm strong

Say nice things to myself

_____

_____

_____

_____

_____

Thinking Like a Scientist

As you know, the stories the mind tells aren't always true, especially when you're feeling anxious and upset.

But anxious thoughts can sure *seem* true. How can you tell which thoughts are fact and which are fiction?

The secret is to **think like a scientist**. That means you think carefully about whether a story is most likely true or false.

A common story the mind can tell is, "It's not safe when I'm away from my parents." That story is almost certainly *fiction*. We know this is true because usually nothing bad happens when you're away from them.

Other stories are *facts*. For example, if the mind says, "You're going to miss your parents," that is probably a true story.

When the mind tells you a story, you can use your **Realize**, **Research**, and **Revise** skills to test out the thought. What is one anxious story you can investigate like a scientist? You can describe it or draw it in the box below.

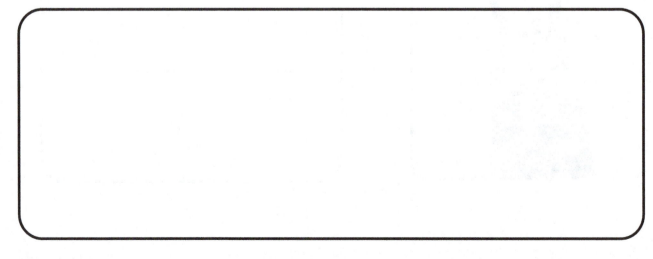

Can Your Mind See the Future?

The mind has lots of ways to make us believe things that aren't true. **Fortune Telling** is one that often makes it harder to be away from family.

The fortunes the mind sees when you're anxious are usually the worst things it can think of.

But these stories almost never come true, so they upset you for no good reason!

You'll know the mind is fortune telling when it says, "I *know* this bad thing is going to happen!"

What is one bad fortune your mind told you that *didn't* come true?

Here are some examples of fortune-telling thoughts that Wei would hear when she was going to school and had to say goodbye to her mom and dad.

You can circle any that sound like stories your own mind has told you!

When you notice your mind is fortune telling,
ask yourself: What is really most likely to happen?

Taking Small Steps to Face Your Fears

The **Be** and **Think** practices can be helpful on their own. But they work extra well when you combine them with **Act** skills like this one!

That's because the fastest way to feel less afraid of something you're afraid to do . . . is to do it!

That's right—nothing teaches your brain to be less afraid than facing what you fear.

It sends a powerful message to your brain: "Maybe this isn't really dangerous."

You won't be facing your fear all at once, as you learned in part 1. You'll start with smaller steps; over time, you can work up to more challenging ones.

8 Sleeping over at a friend's

7 At a friend's without Mom, 4 hours

6 At a friend's without Mom, 2 hours

5 At a friend's without Mom, 1 hour

4 At a friend's with Mom, 1 hour

3 At home while Mom is out a half hour

2 At home while Mom walks around block

1 Playing in my own room

On the left, you'll find Aisha's **courage ladder** for working up to being away from her mom when she plays with friends.

It starts with something that's pretty easy for her: playing by herself in her room while her parents are at home. At the top of her ladder, she'll be able to spend the night at a friend's!

You can create your own courage ladder for facing your fear.

It's a good idea to work with your parents or other adults to find what works for you.

CHAPTER 6

Worrying About Getting Sick

Many people of all ages worry about their health. Some worry about one illness, such as getting cancer. Others worry about all kinds of sicknesses.

Having health worries all the time is upsetting and can make it really hard to enjoy things. Your mind often thinks of the worst when you feel things in your body like a pain in your head or a tickle in your throat.

In this chapter, you'll see how the tools of **Think Act Be** can help.

Releasing the Worry with Each Breath

Once the mind grabs hold of a worry thought, it's not easy to let it go.

It can seem like it's the safe and right thing to hold on to the worry, as if letting go could be dangerous.

It's true that sometimes you'll get sick. **But that doesn't mean you have to live in fear!**

It's not up to you to make sure you *never* get sick. You're allowed to let go of your worries about your health.

You can use your breath and your body to help your mind let go.

1 As you breathe in, make a fist with each of your hands. Imagine that your mind is holding on to this fear in the same way that your hands are squeezing into fists.

2 As you breathe out, relax your hands. Let all the tension drain away. At the same time, feel your mind start to release its tight grip on this worrying thought.

You can repeat this cycle of breathing as often and for as long as you'd like.

Taking a Closer Look at Worst-Case Fears

When the mind is worrying about getting sick, it often goes beyond a simple cold or upset tummy. It imagines the *worst*!

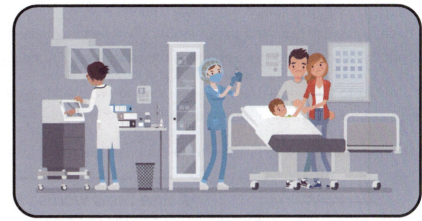

When Blaine heard that a virus was going around, he pictured getting horribly sick from it, even being in the hospital.

What is a worst-case health fear your mind has come up with?

_____

_____

But here's the thing: **The worst thing almost never happens.**

Even when you get sick, it usually turns out okay: You don't feel well, you get the help you need, and you get better.

Blaine ended up catching the virus, and he spent a couple days resting in bed and eating chicken soup. He didn't feel well, but he was not even close to needing to go to the hospital.

Can you revise your mind's worst-case fear to a different story that's more likely to come true?

_____

_____

Remembering What You've Dealt with Already

When you're worried about getting sick, your mind is more likely to think some thoughts than others.

It's really easy for the mind to remember the *worst* sickness you've had or that you've heard about. It's also easy to think about all the sicknesses you *could* get.

It's harder to think of all the times you've been worried but didn't get sick, or the times you got sick and everything turned out fine.

See what comes to mind as you fill in the boxes below.

A time I was worried but didn't get sick:

_____

_____

_____

A time I got sick, but it wasn't too bad:

_____

_____

_____

Someone who was there to help me when I was sick:

_____

_____

_____

What helped me to get through the sickness:

_____

_____

_____

Keep these things in mind when you're feeling anxious about your health. Picture yourself having everything you need to feel strong and healthy again!

CHAPTER 7

Feeling Anxious Around Others

If you sometimes feel nervous around other people, you're not alone! Social anxiety is really common.

You might find it hard to meet new people. Maybe you're really uncomfortable speaking in front of a class. Or you might worry about people making fun of you or thinking you're "weird."

Whatever your anxiety is like, we're going to work on ways to feel more comfortable so that anxiety doesn't control you. With practice, you can face these situations with more confidence and less fear.

Mind Reading Is Harder Than It Looks

I'll bet you know that you can't read someone's mind. But the brain often acts like it can! **Mind Reading** is one of the brain's tricks that leads to social anxiety.

It might tell you that the other students are thinking bad things about you. Or maybe it says to you, "They hate your backpack."

But guess what? Most of the time, other people aren't thinking bad things about you. They're probably not thinking of you at all!

When was a time that your own brain was mind reading? You can write what it told you below. This is step 1 in **Realize, Research, Revise.**

Now let's take a closer look at how you knew they were thinking that. Was there good evidence for it? For example, did they actually say it to you in words? Was there evidence *against* it, like it was only an assumption the brain made?

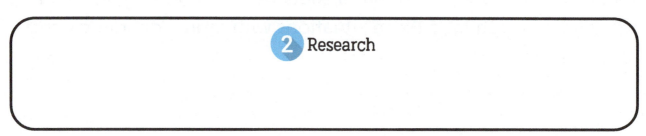

Okay, last step—**Revise**! If the thought wasn't completely right, come up with a truer thought to take its place.

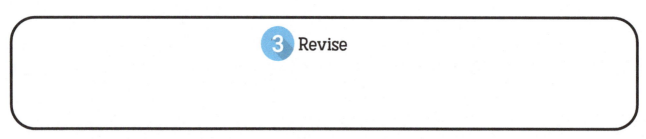

Taking the Spotlight Off of Yourself

Think about a time when you were feeling anxious around other people. Picture that scene as clearly as you can: where you were, what you were doing, who was there.

Now, think about where your attention was. How much of it was shining on how *you* were doing versus on how *others* were doing? You can circle your answer below.

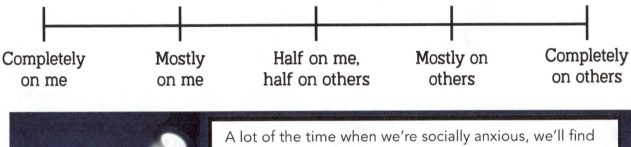

Completely on me   Mostly on me   Half on me, half on others   Mostly on others   Completely on others

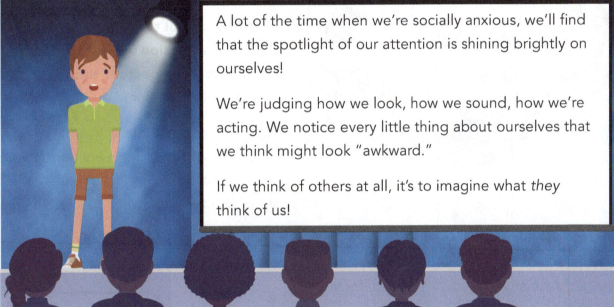

A lot of the time when we're socially anxious, we'll find that the spotlight of our attention is shining brightly on ourselves!

We're judging how we look, how we sound, how we're acting. We notice every little thing about ourselves that we think might look "awkward."

If we think of others at all, it's to imagine what *they* think of us!

See what it's like to shift your attention outside of yourself.

Really notice the people around you.

See where you are.

Be curious about all that's happening that has nothing to do with you!

You can use the box on the right to come up with things you can practice shining the spotlight on, as you take it off yourself!

I can notice:

_____

_____

_____

_____

_____

Making Friends with Anxious Feelings

It's an uncomfortable feeling to be anxious around other people. No wonder we want those feelings to go away!

But having some anxiety around others is very normal. It's something most humans experience.

I feel awkward. I wonder what everyone thinks of me.

Trying to get rid of anxious feelings usually doesn't work. In fact, it often makes things worse.

When we turn anxiety into a problem to get rid of, we just make things harder for ourselves. **All that focus on anxiety takes our attention away from things that are more important to us**, like our friends and having fun!

Instead of trying to make it stop, you can start to make friends with your anxiety whenever it shows up. Making friends starts with telling yourself a different story about it.

Luis came up with some new ways of thinking about his own anxiety around people. You can circle any that you want to try for yourself.

What else might you say to remind yourself that it's okay to feel anxious?

I can tell myself that:

_____

_____

_____

_____

It's *okay* to feel anxious.

Other kids are probably feeling anxious, too.

I don't have to get rid of these feelings.

I'm going to invite these feelings to come with me.

I won't let my emotions stop me from having fun!

Doing a Fear Experiment

A big part of overcoming fear around other people is to climb your **courage ladder**.

It can be extra helpful with social anxiety to treat each step of your ladder as a **fear experiment**.

These experiments will help you to compare what you expect in social situations with how they actually go. This process will show your brain when its guesses aren't right and how they need to be changed.

First, you'll create your courage ladder, as you learned to do in chapter 3.

Next, you'll pick a rung from your courage ladder and fill out the box below for that situation. You can add other results you're worried about in the blanks at the bottom. For example, "People will laugh at me," "My face will get red," or "I'll have nothing to say." Then add a rating from 0 to 10 for how good or bad it felt—higher numbers mean it was worse, lower numbers mean it was better.

Result	What I Expected (0–10)	How It Went (0–10)
I'll feel nervous		
It will go badly		

Most of the time you'll probably find that the value in "How It Went" ends up being less than the one in "What I Expected." So while you're climbing your courage ladder, you'll be learning to see when the mind is playing its tricks!

CHAPTER 8

Feeling Fearful at Nighttime

It's not surprising that fear of the dark is so common. There was a time long ago when it was actually unsafe to be out at night. It's hard for humans to see things that could hurt them when it's dark, like wild animals!

Nowadays, the nighttime isn't so dangerous for most of us. But that doesn't mean the fear has gone away. Maybe you have a fear of monsters or ghosts at night. Or maybe it's not any one thing—you just feel afraid.

That fear can make bedtime feel scary, especially sleeping in your room by yourself. It can also get in the way of fun stuff like your friend's sleepover or sleepaway camp.

In this chapter, you'll see how the **Think Act Be** skills from the first half of this book can help to tame your nighttime fears.

Heavy Body, Calming Breath

When you're alone in the dark and your mind is afraid, it can imagine all kinds of things that aren't there. Those fears can **set off the body's alarm**, which makes the danger seem all the more real.

What do you notice in your own body when you're feeling afraid in the dark?

You can circle your answers on the right and write in anything you've felt that isn't listed.

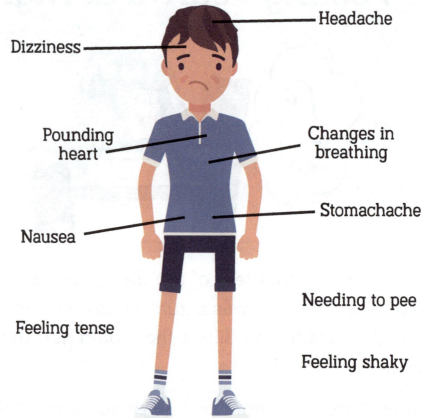

Headache

Dizziness

Pounding heart

Changes in breathing

Stomachache

Nausea

Feeling tense

Needing to pee

Feeling shaky

You can also use the body to help you calm down as you're lying in bed. Let's practice now, before bedtime. That way you'll know what to do at night.

1 Lie down comfortably on the couch or the floor. Put one hand on your belly and the other on your heart.

2 Breathe in gently and feel your belly and chest as they move. Exhale slowly and let all your weight sink down into the floor or couch. Allow your body to be heavy.

3 Keep breathing like this for as long as you like or until you fall asleep. Feel your body becoming a little calmer and heavier with each breath.

What Would You Tell a Good Friend?

Being by yourself in the dark can feel very lonely. But you're never completely alone, even if no one else is close by. Remember that you can be there for yourself.

Being there for yourself means you treat yourself like a friend.

You give yourself the support you need.

You can tell yourself the things you need to hear, like, "I know it's not easy. But you can do this!"

What would you want a good friend to tell you when you're alone and afraid at night?

I would want my friend to tell me that:

_____

_____

_____

_____

You can say the same things to yourself at night.

The love you show yourself as a friend doesn't have to be in words. If you want to, you can even give yourself a hug! Offer yourself the love you need.

Letting Thoughts Drift By

One good way to handle scary thoughts is to really study them and see if they're true. That's what you learned with the skill of **Realize, Research, Revise**.

But there's another way to deal with thoughts. **You can just let them go by**, without giving them a lot of attention.

It doesn't even matter what the actual thoughts are. You treat each one the same, just letting them pass like leaves floating down a stream.

You can practice right now with this exercise. With your eyes closed, imagine a beautiful flowing stream. The water is clear and cold.

There are small leaves floating peacefully downstream. Picture each one of your thoughts floating away like those leaves.

With each breath out, you watch the thoughts come and go.

You can use this skill at night when scary thoughts show up. A thought appears, you notice it, and then it *leaves* (🍁 ha ha). Each thought has no more weight than a single leaf as you let them drift by.

Facing Your Fears to Make Them Shrink

There are lots of ways to face your fear of the dark. On the right, you can see one of the courage ladders that Sasha used to face his own fear.

Sasha was learning to be more comfortable in a dark room. He started by being in the room with his mom or dad for 5 minutes. Over time, he worked up to spending 15 minutes in the room with one of them.

With more practice, he was able to stay in the dark room while his dad was out in the hall, first for 5 minutes and then for longer. Later on, Sasha was in the room while his parents were farther away downstairs.

As you build your own **courage ladder**, you can make the rungs harder or easier by changing things like:

- How long you stay
- How dark the room is
- If you are alone or with someone
- How close by a parent is
- Indoors or outdoors
- Playing a game or just sitting

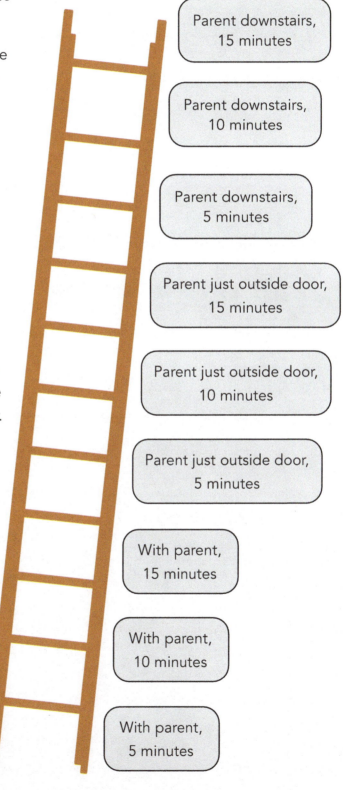

Parent downstairs, 15 minutes

Parent downstairs, 10 minutes

Parent downstairs, 5 minutes

Parent just outside door, 15 minutes

Parent just outside door, 10 minutes

Parent just outside door, 5 minutes

With parent, 15 minutes

With parent, 10 minutes

With parent, 5 minutes

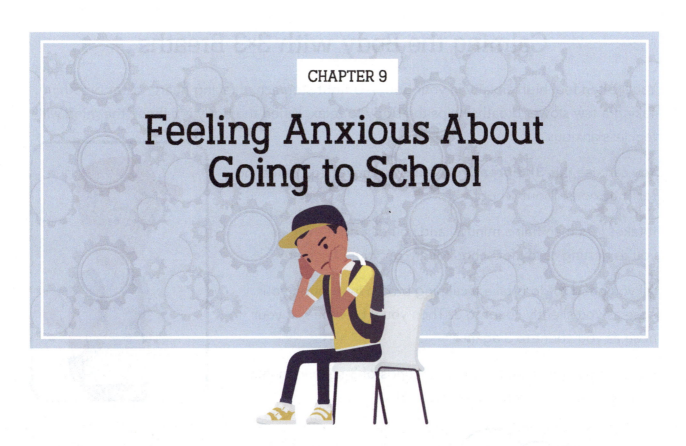

CHAPTER 9

Feeling Anxious About Going to School

There are different reasons that people feel anxious about going to school. If you don't have a lot of friends there, it can feel lonely and not very fun.

Being away from your home and family might also be hard. Or sometimes the anxiety and worry are about schoolwork, like if you have a test that you don't feel ready for.

There can even be anxiety about anxiety itself! If school is a place where your heart pounds, your body shakes, and you feel unsafe, you might worry about how anxious you'll feel.

Let's explore the tools that can make school less scary. These skills can help not only with feeling more comfortable but with lowering the conflict you might be having with your parents about going to school.

Calming the Body with 3×3 Breaths

You'll often feel high anxiety in your body—a tight stomach, a racing heart, faster breathing. Taking a few slower breaths helps the body to relax. When the body is calmer, the mind will feel less anxious.

You can use this **3×3 breath exercise** whenever you're feeling really anxious about school.

It takes less than half a minute, and you can do it even as you're getting ready for school or are on your way there.

All you need to do is take a calming breath in through your nose as you silently count to 3. Then you'll breathe out your nose as you count to 3 again.

Repeat twice more for a total of 3 rounds of 3-second inhales and exhales—that's what makes it 3×3!

In . . . 1 . . . 2 . . . 3, out . . . 1 . . . 2 . . . 3

You don't have to *try* to feel less anxious. Just know that each breath is melting away a little bit of anxiety while you keep getting ready.

One powerful way to use this skill is to do it *before* your anxiety feels out of control.

You can do a few rounds at different times during your morning routine—for example, while you're getting dressed, eating breakfast, and packing your book bag.

You'll also bring your breath with you, so you can use the 3x3 exercise anytime throughout the day!

Questioning the Mind's Scary Stories

Your thoughts about school can lead to anxiety. But your anxiety can also affect your thoughts! One of the mind's favorite tricks is **Thinking with Feelings**.

When you think with feelings, you let your emotions tell you what is true. That means if you *feel* anxious about school, you might *think* something bad is going to happen.

For example, when Noor felt anxious about a test at school, he thought it wasn't going to go well.

What was something at school that you felt anxious about recently?

In what ways did your feelings affect how you thought things were going to go?

Be on the lookout for the **Thinking with Feelings** trick when you're anxious about school. You can use your **Realize, Research, Revise** skills to notice when the mind is playing this trick!

Leaning Into the Unknown Day Ahead

These kinds of unknowns about school can be scary. The mind is good at filling in the blanks with lots of stories about things that could go wrong.

No wonder we might want to run away from the unknown! But as we've seen, **fear grows when we run from it**. The truth is that most of the things we worry about won't come true. Best of all, the unknown is also where all the *good* surprises live!

Think of any good thing in your life—your friends, the games you love, a pet if you have one, and everything else. They all used to be unknowns!

So instead of fleeing from the unknown, **see how you can lean in**. For example, Michael wasn't sure if he would find someone to play with at recess. He leaned into that unknown by going to recess and seeing what kinds of games kids were playing and how he might join in.

Take a few moments now to think of an unknown about your school day. Notice how you feel. Then take a calm, steady breath and find that strong and peaceful place inside you. Now ask yourself, "How can I lean into this unknown?"

You can write down or draw what you come up with in the box below.

My unknown:	How to lean in:

Putting One Foot in Front of the Other

Seeing the whole school day in front of you can feel like too much. It's hard to hold in your mind all that you'll need to deal with: friends, teachers, lunch, tests, and lots more.

But here's the secret: You only need to do *one* thing at a time. Just one. And you can handle that one thing! You have a fantastic ability to solve the problem that's right in front of you.

All you need to do is what you're doing right now.

If you're getting dressed, all you need to do is put on your clothes.

If you're having breakfast, all you need to do is eat your Cheerios.

If you're learning new ideas in math, all you need to do is be right there in the classroom.

You can start putting one foot in front of the other, one step at a time, as you're getting ready for school.

What are the small steps you take each morning that make up your morning routine?

Start your day with little steps and let them carry you through everything you do!

Step-by-step morning plan:

1. _____

2. _____

3. _____

4. _____

5. _____

CHAPTER 10

Feeling Worried All the Time

It's no fun to worry, especially when it won't stop! It can start with anything you care about when you don't know how it's going to turn out.

It could be about your school day or your health. Maybe your mind worries about the weather, your family, or if you're going to get lost. Whatever it's about, the mind imagines what could go wrong and asks, "What if _____?" *What if no one talks to me at school? What if my dad forgets to pick me up?*

When one worry goes away, another often takes its place. All the anxiety that comes with worry can lead to tension in your body, anger toward the people around you, and poor sleep. Let's look at how you can get a break from all this worry.

Calming Breaths to Help You Be Right Here

Worry takes you out of the present and into your imagination about the future. When you notice your mind asking, "What if . . . ?" follow these simple steps.

1 Bring your attention to your breath. Take a slow breath in, and an even *slower* breath out. Your breath helps you come back to where you really are.

I am here . . .

5 You can come back to this exercise no matter what you're doing. Whatever is going on, you are right where you are!

2 As you breathe in again, think to yourself the words, "I am . . ."

As you breathe out, think to yourself, ". . . here."

4 Repeat these 3 words with your breath as many times as you like. Let it be easy—you don't need to force anything. Your brain and body know what to do.

3 Let this silent message to yourself bring your attention to where you are and to what is actually happening. Right here and now, things are probably okay.

Inviting Worry Along for the Ride

Worry can get in the way of doing fun things. For example, Juan had a lot of worries about getting sick. When his friends asked him to come to the park and play basketball, a part of him really wanted to go.

But another part wasn't sure it was a good idea. What if one of his friends had a cold and passed it on to him? It felt *safer* just to stay home.

Juan decided to play with his friends even though he was worried. He was pretty nervous at first, but before long, he was having a good time. His worries didn't seem like the most important thing when he was having fun with his buddies.

When you're worried and anxious, you can still do things you enjoy. Invite worry to "come along for the ride."

If you wait until you're not worried, you'll miss out on a lot of good things. On the other hand, **getting involved in an activity can help you start to forget about your worries**.

What are 3 things you enjoy that you could do when you're worried?

Even when I'm worrying, I can:

1 _____

2 _____

3 _____

Letting Go of Arguments with Worry

Being stuck in worry is a lot like having an argument you can't win. On one side of the worry argument is the fear that something bad will happen. "What if I forget my lunch?" "What if there's no bathroom on the playground?"

The other side is when you try to think through the problem and "solve it" in your head.

Let's say you're worried about a math test. The fear asks, "What if I don't know the answers? What if I run out of time?"

Those thoughts trigger anxiety, so you might try to **work out the problem in your head** to make sure the test goes okay.

Maybe you remind yourself that you studied well and that you get good grades in math. You might feel a little calmer for a while. But then the worry starts again! "But what if . . . " The mind *knows* there's still a chance something will go wrong, so it keeps telling you that there could be a problem.

Things to say when the mind asks "What if?"

- That's possible.
- I guess I'll wait and see.
- I can't be 100% sure that won't happen!
- I'll deal with it if it does.
- That's not something I can control.
- That would become a new problem to solve!

You can't make all the what-ifs go away. But you *can* choose not to argue with worry.

Instead of trying to tell the worry that things will be okay, start to let the what-ifs be there. You don't have to fight them.

You can even go along with them! When worry asks, "What if?" you can answer, "Sure, that might happen. And if it does, I'll handle it then."

Retrain your brain and reclaim your peace of mind!

Seeing Yourself Handle Anything That Happens

The worry mind has a great imagination! It's really good at thinking of all sorts of problems that could pop up.

What is something that the worried part of your brain is telling you might happen? You can describe it with words or draw a picture in the box below.

Most of the time your worries don't come true. **And even if they do, you have an amazing ability to take care of problems!** But here's the thing: The worry mind doesn't have a great imagination for all the ways you could handle the problems it worries about.

In the box to the right, write or draw how you could deal with the thing you're worried might happen.

You can include any grown-ups you might ask for help.

It also helps to remember all the problems you've already solved. You still carry inside you the strengths that helped you to handle those problems.

Saying Goodbye to Mental Control

We can't solve a problem by "thinking at" it! But that's exactly what the mind tries to do when we worry. It wants to make sure things will be okay by thinking through all the bad things that could happen.

It's a lot like someone who is flying on a plane and trying to keep it in the air with their mind! They know the pilot is in charge of the airplane, but they keep a close eye and ear on how things are going.

They could just read a book or take a nap, and the plane would keep flying all the same. But their mind thinks it has to keep a lookout for danger.

When the plane lands safely, the mind sees that it worried and things went okay . . . so it thinks worry must work! "Good thing you worried," it says.

But the truth is that **your mind doesn't have that kind of power**. Worry doesn't keep planes in the air, or stop us from getting sick, or change anything that's outside our control.

You can start to question the belief that you *need* to worry. You're allowed to live your life without trying to solve the future!

Knowing you don't have to worry doesn't make the worry go away. But it *can* help to loosen the mind's grip on worries.

What can you tell yourself as a reminder that it's not your job to worry?

I can tell myself that:

_____

_____

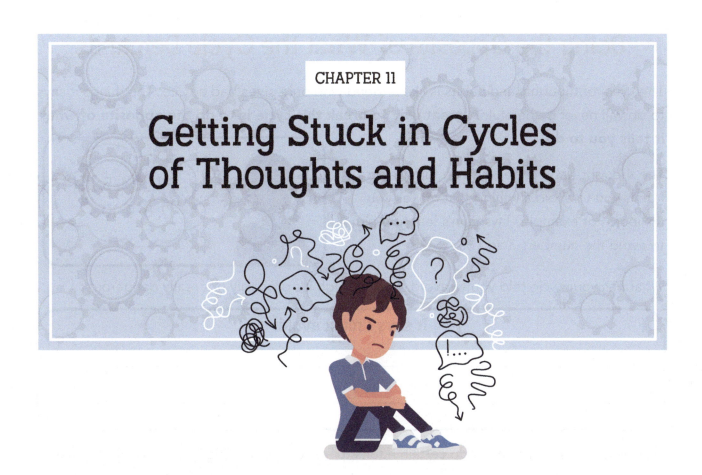

CHAPTER 11

Getting Stuck in Cycles of Thoughts and Habits

When the mind thinks of something bad that might happen, it makes sense that you want to make sure things will be okay and get rid of the bad feeling. You might think or do something to cancel out the thought or fear and to be sure everyone stays safe.

But a lot of the time, these thoughts and habits aren't helpful. For example, you might wash your hands, then worry that they're still dirty and wash them again many times. Or you think a "bad" thought and have to do something over and over until you think the "right" one.

This cycle can be powerful, and hard to break. The skills you'll be learning in this chapter can stop the cycle and make you feel free again.

Doing the Opposite of What the Cycle Demands

The cycle of thoughts and habits is like a friend who only gives bad advice. The things it says to do will never be helpful. **A great way to break this cycle is to do the opposite of what it tells you to do!**

The thought/habit cycle says two things. First, it tells you to *avoid* anything that makes you anxious. For example, Tayshaun's fear told him to avoid the numbers 3 and 6.

What has your cycle told you to avoid, even though it's probably not really dangerous?

> ### It says I must avoid:
>
> _____
>
> _____

The cycle also says you *must* do certain habits to make sure nothing bad happens. Tayshaun always thought he had to say a special prayer to cancel out thinking of 3 or 6.

What has your own cycle told you that you have to do?

> ### It says I have to:
>
> _____
>
> _____

The skills in this chapter will help you to do the opposite of what the cycle demands of you.

It won't always be easy, but it's also not easy feeling like you don't control your thoughts and actions!

The more you practice, the easier it will be to ignore the voice of the cycle and feel okay as you do.

Saying No to Unhelpful Habits

It's easy to see how the scary thoughts you have lead to the habits you do. But it's also true that the habits lead to more scary thoughts.

The thought/habit cycle is like a dog that barks for a treat. When you have a scary thought, the cycle says, "BARK BARK BARK!" which means, "Do a habit to keep things safe!" If you do the habit, it might quiet down.

But here's the problem: When you quiet a barking dog by giving her a treat, you're training her to come back for more treats! So every time the cycle feels "hungry" for a habit, it will BARK BARK BARK until you do one.

The fear dog is also training *you* to do more habits when you feel afraid. When you feel a little better after a habit, you've learned that habits bring relief from fear and anxiety. You'll start to believe that you can feel better *only* by doing habits.

Fear leads to habits, and habits lead to more fear.

The solution is to stop feeding the fear dog. That means when the cycle barks, you say "no" to unhelpful habits. This may be hard, because what does a dog do when she barks but doesn't get a treat? She barks louder! So the fear might feel stronger at first.

Remember not to feed the fear dog when it barks louder. Giving in would teach it that barking louder will make you do what it wants!

If you refuse to do those habits even when it's hard, the fear will go down naturally. With practice, your mind will learn to be less afraid and that you don't need to do the habits to be okay.

The best way to feel less fear is to stop the habits *and* to face the things your fear says to avoid, as you'll see next.

Facing Your Triggers One Step at a Time

Your **courage ladder** will help you climb out of fear and into freedom. (See chapter 3 if you need to review.) The things on your ladder might be real-life places or objects, such as touching doorknobs or wearing a shirt you feel is "unlucky." You might also have fears about saying or even thinking certain words or numbers.

It's best to face all the things on your courage ladder to overcome your fears. But, of course, not all at once! You'll begin as always with the lower rungs on your ladder. If you try to go too fast, you may not be able to stop yourself from doing the habits you want to break.

It's really important while you're climbing that you **don't do the habits that the cycle is asking for**. That way you'll be doing the opposite of everything it wants.

Facing fears but still doing the habits to feel better is like climbing your courage ladder and then climbing back down! So slow and steady is usually the best way to face your fears.

Check out the table below for some examples of how to face fears. Some might look familiar, and some may not apply to you at all.

Examples of How to Face Fears		
Scary Thought	**What the Cycle Says to Do**	**What to Do**
"That doorknob has germs on it."	"Don't touch it!"	Touch the doorknob
"9 is an unlucky number."	"Avoid the number 9."	Think, say, and write "9"
"Something bad will happen if I don't line up my sneakers."	"Make sure your sneakers are lined up right."	Leave the sneakers looking wrong
"God will punish me if I think that."	"Don't ever think that."	Think and/or write the thought
"My mom will get sick if I wear that shirt."	"You must never wear that shirt."	Wear the shirt

Being the Observer of Thoughts and Feelings

You'll learn something big while you're doing the opposite of what the cycle wants: **Thoughts and feelings don't have to drive your actions.**

 You can feel afraid and still choose not to do a habit.

 You can face the things that make you feel afraid.

You can have a scary thought and choose to ignore it.

You can have a "bad thought" and just keep going with your day.

You can always **use your breath** to help you just observe what's happening in your mind and body.

Slow down your breath when thoughts and feelings are upsetting.

Find the calm inside you—the peaceful place when storms are all around.

The fear and upset will rise like a wave, reach their highest point, and then come down again.

Remember that you don't need to react. The scary feelings will just fade away.

117

II. Working Through Challenging Emotions

CHAPTER 12

Feeling Sad and Down

All of us have ups and downs in how we feel. If something doesn't go well, we feel sad. We feel happy when we get a nice surprise.

But maybe you've been feeling down for a while now. You might feel sad and low for most of the day. Maybe you don't feel like doing any activities, even the ones that used to be fun.

A low mood can also affect your sleep and appetite, along with how you feel about yourself. It can make it seem like you have nothing to look forward to.

But these rough patches don't last forever, and the right tools will help you start to feel better. So take a nice, easy breath, and let's see how this works.

Taking Action to Lift Your Spirits

Your feelings and the things you do are closely tied together. When you're sad, down, or feeling blue, you might not really feel like doing much. Your energy is probably low, and nothing sounds all that fun.

For these reasons, it's common to start doing fewer activities. You might not get together with your friends as much or do your favorite things. It's probably harder to take care of things like chores and homework, too.

Are there activities you're less interested in doing when you're feeling down?

If you stop doing many fun and important things, you won't be getting the good feelings that come from those activities. That means your mood will drop even lower . . . which makes it even harder to do activities!

This is called a **vicious cycle**, when the first unhelpful thing leads to a second unhelpful thing, which leads to *more* of the first thing, and you feel worse and worse.

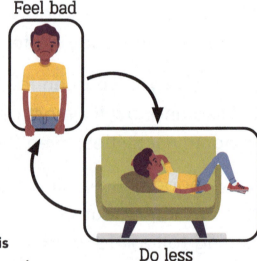

Feel bad

Do less

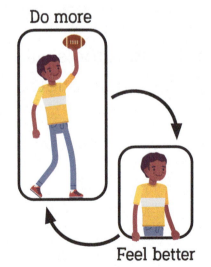

Do more

Feel better

The way to break this cycle is to start with action. You have more direct control over what you *do* than over how you *feel*.

You can find a step-by-step plan for doing more fun and important things in chapter 3. As you follow the plan, your mood will start to feel brighter. When your mood improves, it gets easier to do things.

You can start to feel better pretty quickly once you get the wheels moving in a good direction. Now you'll be in a **virtuous cycle**, where good things lead to more good things!

Changing Your Mind to Change Your Feelings

Your thoughts can play a big part in how you feel. When you're already feeling low, your mind will think of even more things that bring you down.

It will be using its favorite **tricks**—those "glasses" that make you see things that aren't there or miss things that are. These tricks will often be about the way you see yourself and your life. Here are three to look out for.

Mind Trick	Example	New Thought
All-or-Nothing Thinking	"Zoë doesn't want to play with me. Nobody likes me."	"I have other friends who will want to play with me."
Magnifying	"I missed a goal. I'm terrible at soccer."	"Even the best pros don't make all their shots."
Ignoring the Positive	"The party got rained out. Nothing good ever happens."	"I get to go over to my friend's house today instead."

Changing thoughts that aren't true can go a long way toward feeling better and not being so down on yourself. The **Realize, Research, Revise** exercise from chapter 2 can be really helpful for spotting these tricks and not being fooled by them.

Breathing with Whatever You're Feeling

Changing thoughts and actions can do a lot to lift your mood. But we can't "fix" every feeling. You may feel better but still feel a bit down. Even if you feel well again, there will be times when you don't feel so great.

Whatever the cause may be, **your breath is here for you**. It offers comfort when things seem too hard. It brings you back to that still place inside, that center where peace can always be found.

But don't believe it just because I said so! Take a moment now to see what it's like for yourself.

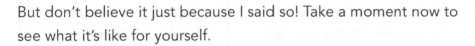

Close your eyes (or keep them open if you want).

Feel your body right where you're sitting.

Now take a slow breath in, sensing the lungs as they fill with air.

As you breathe out slowly, just notice any emotions you feel.

As you breathe in, feel your breath expand the body, making as much space as you need to hold all your feelings.

Whatever the emotions are, you can say to yourself, "This is how I feel right now. It's part of being human. And it's okay to feel how I feel."

Keep breathing with your feelings for as long as you like.

Something big can happen from the practice of making room for feelings: They start to feel less upsetting. They might still be there, but somehow, they don't feel quite as bad.

The breath is yours to turn to as often as you need it.

CHAPTER 13

Feeling Tense and Stressed

Whenever you have to deal with a problem, your body turns on a kind of alarm to help you handle it. The alarm turns on when you're in danger and need to run away, when you want to perform well on a test, during a big game or a concert, when you're sick and need to heal, or when any other problem comes up.

It's an amazing and well-built system. But it doesn't feel good when there's too much stress in your life and the alarm is on all the time. Your body might start to feel tense, you may get stomachaches or headaches, and you just want a break from it all.

In this chapter, you'll learn ways to find some rest from lots of stress. We'll begin with the *thoughts* that can make stress worse.

Releasing Thoughts That Crank Up Stress

Stress isn't "all in your head." It's based on your brain and body's response to difficult, exciting, or challenging things. But your thoughts can make these things feel even more stressful! Here's how to deal with some common thoughts that lead to more stress.

You don't have to do everything all at once. You can make a list and work through it one by one.

Watch out for **Fortune-Telling** thoughts that make you think something bad will happen.

Worries about time can be really stressful. You can't make things take less time than they need!

When you're feeling lots of stress, **pause for just a moment and see what's on your mind**. Remind yourself that the stressful stories aren't always true. Is there another way of seeing things that is truer and more helpful? You can create your own scene below for a stressful thought you tell yourself!

Stress thought:

Helpful thought:

Taking Care of What Is Stressing You Out

Having a lot to do can be stressful. But not doing what you need to can create even more stress. It's not fun to see things piling up when you know you need to take care of them.

For example, Grace fell behind in her math workbook. Every time she thought about all the pages she needed to do, she got a sick feeling.

"I have to do it, but it's too much!" she thought to herself. She worried that she'd never get it done.

Are there things you've been putting off that you know you need to do? You can write them in the box to the right.

The trick for getting things done, as we've seen before, is to **make them small and easy**. Little steps will let you reach a big goal.

Things I need to do:

_____

_____

_____

_____

_____

Grace realized she didn't have to do all 15 pages of homework in one night. She could do 3 pages each night from Monday to Friday, and then she'd be done.

There are many ways to make your tasks easier, as we saw in chapter 3. You can look back to that chapter if you need to review.

How could you break one of your own tasks into small steps to help you get it done?

Step 1: _____

Step 2: _____

Step 3: _____

Step 4: _____

Step 5: _____

Doing Things That Bring You Joy

Stress has a way of emptying you out. It takes mental, physical, and emotional energy to handle difficult things, and it can leave you feeling drained, like an empty bucket.

Doing things you enjoy takes your mind off the stresses you're dealing with, so you get a break from them. Here are some activity ideas. Just find the things that work for you!

With Friends

Kick a soccer ball
Play board games
Write a story together
Do art projects
Explore your backyard

With Family

Go to the pool
Play in a park
Watch a movie together
Dance to music
Bake cookies

Alone

Read a book
Solve a crossword puzzle
Shoot a basketball
Make an obstacle course
Play dress-up

What are three things you like to do that could fill your bucket when you're feeling stressed?

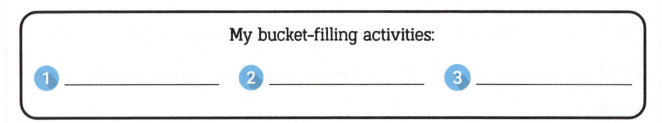

My bucket-filling activities:

1 _____   2 _____   3 _____

Finding Peace in the Breath

Your breath can be a powerful tool to decrease stress. This exercise will help you use your breath to **find peace when you're stressed**.

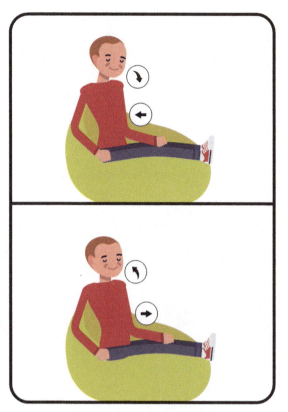

1 Find a comfortable place to sit, away from noise and people if possible.

Let your eyes close if that helps you to focus.

2 Next, let your breath be slow and calm.

Feel your belly rise when you breathe in and fall as you breathe out.

3 Count 10 of these slow, gentle breaths: On the first exhale, silently say, "1." On the second exhale, say, "2," and so forth.

It's fine if you lose count! You can start again from the last number you remember counting.

4 If you like, you can breathe out through your mouth with a loud sigh: "Ahhhh . . ." Feel the stress leave your body with each sigh.

When you reach 10, pause for a moment and notice how you feel. You can return to this breath practice whenever you need to.

Feeling Bored, Bored, Bored

CHAPTER 14

All of your toys or books seem dull. There's no one to play with, nothing interesting to do, no fun activities. You've got that *blah* feeling that comes with being bored.

Everyone feels bored at times. Waiting in line or at the doctor's office. Being stuck in a long meeting or service. Listening to adults chatting on and on about grown-up stuff. It's a painful feeling, right?

We'll never get rid of boredom once and for all, and this chapter explores why maybe that's not such a bad thing. But as you'll see, there are ways to make being bored less painful.

Becoming a Boredom-ologist

Being bored is . . . boring, right? You probably hate how it feels when there's nothing interesting happening.

What are the worst parts about being bored?

1 _____

2 _____

3 _____

4 _____

But here's the thing: **Boredom itself can actually be pretty interesting, when you really get to know it!**

The next time you're feeling bored, study it like you're a boredom scientist.

Fill in the boxes below with your new discoveries about boredom:

What is actually happening around you right now? No detail is too small.	How would you describe boredom to someone who'd never experienced it?	Where in your body do you feel boredom? Are the feelings always the same or do they vary?
_____	_____	_____
_____	_____	_____
_____	_____	_____
_____	_____	_____
_____	_____	_____
_____	_____	_____

Creating a Boredom List

When you're feeling bored, it's harder to think of things to do. Plan ahead by **creating a list of things you can do when you're feeling bored**.

It helps to include things you can do alone and things to do with others, like a sibling or a friend. The alone activities are good when no one is around (or willing!) to play with you.

It's also best to have things on your list that you can do without an adult's help. For example, it wouldn't be good to only list things that you need a parent to drive you to!

You can start your list now and add new things to it whenever you think of them. Use a blank piece of paper that you can keep somewhere that it's easy to find when you need it.

When you pull out your list for something to do, you can choose whatever sounds good to you.

You can also see what it's like to pick something randomly: Close your eyes, put your finger down on your list, and then do whatever it lands on!

Even if you don't feel like doing the activity you pick, you can go ahead and get started on it. **Feeling interested in something often comes while you're *doing* it, not when you're *thinking* about doing it**.

Turning Boredom Into a Gift for Someone Else

There's a really stuck feeling to being bored. Nothing sounds interesting, and it's hard to think of any way to make things better.

One good way to break out of this stuckness is to play a different kind of game. Instead of asking yourself how you can stop feeling bored, you can **look for something kind to do for someone else**.

Think about who around you could use a little help. How could you make their day better or easier?

When Bennie was bored, he chose to make a card for his friend Fernando, who had been sick. It was a relief to stop focusing on his own feelings and to think about his friend.

It's usually easier to start by thinking of what someone you know might need, rather than trying to think of something that you *feel* like doing. If you focus on your feelings, you'll probably run into the same old problem of feeling bored and uninterested in anything you think of doing!

Gift ideas for others:

Make them a snack

Do one of their chores

Pick them some flowers

Write them a nice note

There are all kinds of ways to turn your boredom into someone else's gift. The box to the left has some ideas to get you started.

You can add any ideas you have to your boredom list.

What is one act of kindness you could do for someone else?

_____

_____

When you shift to thinking of others, a funny thing often happens. You wind up feeling a lot better without even trying to! Showing care to someone turns out to be a gift you give yourself.

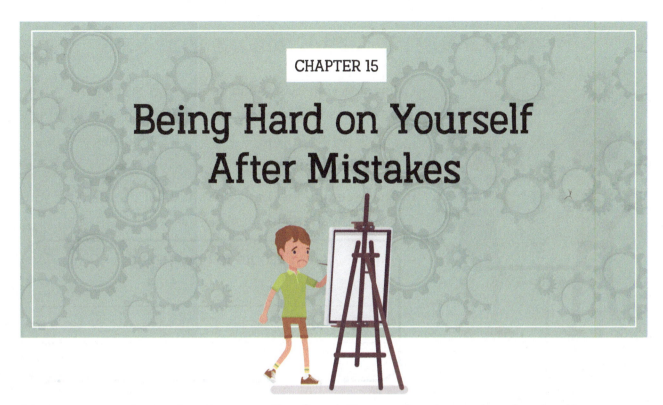

CHAPTER 15

Being Hard on Yourself After Mistakes

Humans make mistakes—all of us! Even the best basketball players sometimes miss a free throw. Graceful skaters slip and fall. Teachers misspeak in front of the class.

But when the mistake is your own, it can be harder to accept it and bounce back. You might feel really upset with yourself for singing at the wrong time in a choral concert or think you're "no good" at a school subject because you got a question wrong.

The skills in this chapter can make it easier to be okay with making a mistake. You'll learn that it doesn't mean something bad about you, and that you can always try again.

Maybe best of all, you can find more courage to try new things so that a fear of mistakes doesn't hold you back.

Treating Yourself Like Someone You Like

Imagine your best friend comes over and you're having a snack together. When your friend refills their cup of water, they pour too much by mistake and it overflows onto the table.

They seem to feel bad about it. What do you think you would say to them?

> **I would tell my friend:**
>
> _____
>
> _____

Now imagine the same scene, but this time *you* pour yourself too much water and it spills on the table. What do you think you would say to yourself if this happened?

> **I would say to myself:**
>
> _____
>
> _____

Take a look at your two answers. Most likely you had a different reaction to your friend than to yourself in exactly the same situation. We tend to be kind to someone we like when they mess up, and harder on ourselves.

What could you think to treat yourself like someone you like? You can fill in the thought bubble to the right. It can help to imagine what you would say to a friend.

All of us make mistakes. It's easier to bounce back from them when we show ourselves a little kindness!

Growing Through Mistakes

What does it say about you when you make a mistake? The mind often thinks the worst, like that there's something "wrong" with you or that you'll always make the same mistake.

But anyone who ever learned something made mistakes along the way! And even once they know how to do it, they're not perfect. **Mistakes will happen.**

For example, Ryan's dad was teaching him how to make scrambled eggs. When Ryan tried to crack an egg into the bowl, the egg ended up on the counter instead!

Did this mistake mean that Ryan would never be good at cracking eggs? Of course not! He's still learning. Making a mess this time will actually help him get *better* at making eggs, because it shows him what to do differently next time.

Watch out for things the mind tells you about what it means to mess up. Look for ways to remind yourself that you're learning and growing. Here are some examples.

Old meaning:	New meaning:
"I'm bad at this."	"I'm getting better."
"I'll never learn how to do this."	"I can improve with practice."
"I shouldn't even try."	"The only way to learn is to do it."
"I must be dumb."	"I'm still learning."

When was a time that you learned from a mistake? You can write about it below.

The mistake I made:	What I learned from it:
_____	_____
_____	_____

Every mistake you make is a chance to grow. Instead of saying mean things to yourself you can ask, "What have I learned that will help me next time?" This way of thinking will remind you that when you make a mistake, you can always try again!

Remembering That Practice Makes . . . Progress

When Sadie got some problems wrong on her math test, she was mad at herself. "I'm no good at math!" she thought. But then she caught herself. "I'm still learning," she realized.

She also thought about what she had told her friend Leo when he missed some questions on a test. "That's okay, you'll get it," she had said. "If I can say that to my friend, maybe I can say it to myself," she thought.

When Sadie was mad at herself and thought she was bad at math, she didn't want to spend time trying to learn. What was the point if she was *never* going to get it?

Her new way of thinking made her more willing to practice, and when she practiced, she got better. Not *perfect*, even though some people say, "Practice makes perfect" (see chapter 19). But really, **practice makes progress**.

It's like riding a bike. At first, you can't do it at all. You start out with training wheels, or a balance bike with no pedals.

Then you start trying to ride a bike, and you fall over. You try again, and you crash. Then you're able to stay up for a few seconds, and then for longer.

Next, you work on starting and stopping till those skills get easier. It's not long before riding your bike feels about as natural as walking. (Which you also had to learn how to do!)

What things have you already learned to do? You can write a few in the box below.

I have learned how to:

_____

_____

_____

Each time you make a mistake, remind yourself that everything you've learned so far came from trying again!

III. Getting Things Done

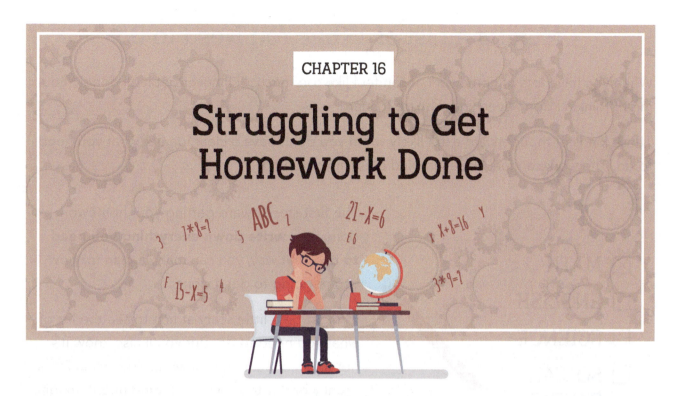

CHAPTER 16

Struggling to Get Homework Done

Homework can be hard for lots of reasons. The ideas might be new and not so clear, and your teacher is not there to explain things.

Sometimes you might have so much of it and you're not sure where to start. And, of course, there are times when you just don't *feel* like doing homework.

No matter what's getting in the way, it probably won't work so well to try to force your way through it. What you need are a few helpful tools that make it easier to get things done.

That's exactly what you'll be learning in this chapter. Let's take a look at the things that can help.

Making a List of What You Need to Do

When you have lots of homework, it can feel like too much. "I'll never get it all done!" you might think. "I don't even know where to start!"

Those kinds of thoughts are extra likely when you don't have a clear idea of what you need to do. The work can feel like a jumbled mess in your mind.

The first step toward getting your homework done is to **write down everything you need to do**. That way, you can make a plan for how you're going to get it done.

It might be a little scary at first to see the list of what you need to do. But you'll also know it's not an *infinite* amount of work. The actual list is usually better than what the mind might imagine.

What does your own homework include? You can write what you need to do in the list to the right.

Something else can happen when you make your list: You start to plan for when you'll do each thing. You might think, "I can do that one this afternoon and that one after dinner. And that's not due till Friday." In other words, **you start to see a path forward**.

You might still feel nervous about the work, but you know that everything you *have to* do is on the list. There are no mystery assignments that are going to jump out at you and say, "Boo!"

My homework list:

_____

_____

_____

_____

_____

_____

And you have other skills you can use to get things done, such as using your breath to deal with difficult feelings about the work, as we'll see next.

Breathing Through the Discomfort

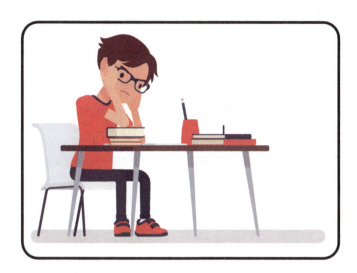

The same amount of homework can look really different based on how you're feeling. When you're anxious and stressed, the work might seem impossible. But when you're feeling calm, it seems easier to do.

Your breath can help you move through tough emotions so you can **do your work with more ease**. Even if the feelings don't go away, you'll be able to do what you need to.

You can start using your breath right when you sit down to do your work. Take a few moments to settle in and breathe nice and easy. Inhale as you count to 3. Exhale as you count to 6. Repeat this in-and-out cycle 3 times.

See how it feels now to take a few rounds of breath like this—in for 3, out for 6. Allow it to be as easy as you can.

You can stay with your breath as you get started on your work. Take things nice and slow to match your breath. Let it carry you through the things you're doing. You can pause and take a couple breaths whenever you start a new assignment or subject.

When you feel your emotions ramping up again, you can also use your breath to bring you back to a calmer place.

Pause your work if you need to, or just notice your breath as you keep working. **You aren't trying to get rid of the feelings.** You're letting your breath carry you through them.

When you finish your work, take a couple more breaths as you thank yourself for all the work you've done!

Breaking It Down Into Bite-Sized Pieces

Small jobs are easier than big jobs. **They take less time, less focus, and less effort.** It's easier to get started on a small job because you know it won't take too long and you have a better idea of how to do it.

Every big homework task is made of a bunch of little ones. Thirty pages of reading breaks down into 3 sections of 10 pages. Twenty-five math problems is 5 sets of 5 problems. Four worksheets is 1 worksheet 4 times.

When your homework feels like too much, break it down into bite-sized pieces to help yourself get through it. The list of homework you made is a first step in breaking things down.

You can go a step further and break down each assignment into smaller parts.

For example, Ari had to write a report on the water cycle. The whole report felt too big, like trying to eat a whole burger in one bite!

So Ari split that big project into 3 smaller ones: doing his research, making an outline, and writing the paper. Each step felt like taking a right-sized bite.

You can use the boxes below to break down one of your own homework assignments.

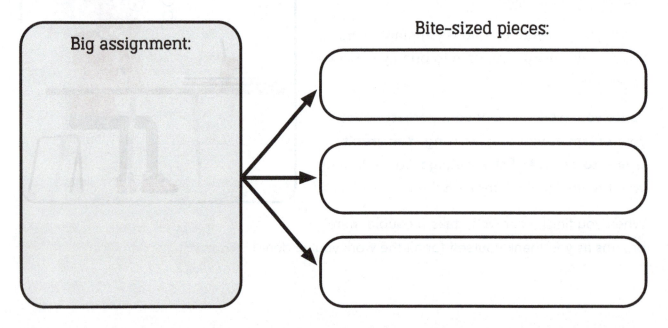

Big assignment:

Bite-sized pieces:

Changing Thoughts That Make Work Harder

As you're doing your work, notice if your thoughts are making it harder or easier.

Unhelpful thoughts tell you you're *never* going to get it done, or that you're going to do badly on it. They might also tell you that you're not smart enough to understand something or to learn a new skill.

These kinds of thoughts can fill you with anxiety or make you feel like giving up, and they make it harder to do your work.

What unhelpful thought has your mind told you when you were trying to do homework?

_____

_____

On the other hand, **more useful thoughts lower anxiety, make the work easier, and help you finish it**. They also don't use the mind tricks you've learned about, such as **Thinking with Feelings** or **Fortune Telling**.

Emily found herself thinking she would never learn her times tables. But then she took a closer look at that thought. "That's not true," she realized. "I've already learned some of them, and I'll keep practicing till I know them."

What is a more helpful thought you can tell yourself to help you do your homework?

_____

_____

You can practice saying this thought to yourself as you sit down to start your work. That way your mind will be working *for* you right from the beginning!

Doing Exactly What You Need to Do

Once you're ready to start working, it's helpful to focus on what you're actually doing. Focusing helps you do your best work. You aren't distracted by other things, and all of your mental energy goes toward what you're doing.

Right now, I'm *only* doing math.

When your mind thinks of all the other things it needs to do, let it know that there will be time for those things, then gently bring your attention back to what you're doing. **You can only do one thing at a time**, so anything else you need to do will just have to wait its turn!

What helps you focus on what you're doing, and what makes it harder to focus?

Helps me focus:	Makes it harder to focus:
_____	_____
_____	_____

You might need to clean your workspace, too. Put away the books and folders you aren't using at the moment. You only need to have out the one thing you're working on.

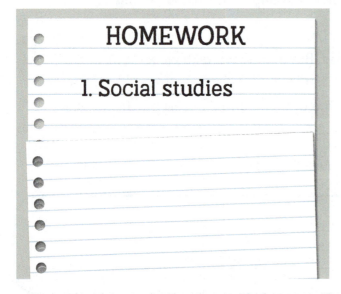

HOMEWORK

1. Social studies

It can help to hide all the other tasks on your list so you're seeing only the one you're doing.

For example, Lily uses another piece of paper to cover the things lower on her homework list. That way, she doesn't keep seeing other tasks and feeling nervous about getting them done.

Whatever you're working on, this is *it*! You'll finish *every*thing by doing *one* thing at a time.

CHAPTER 17

Feeling Unhappy About Doing Chores

As you get older, you'll have more things your parents expect you to take care of: cleaning your room, clearing the table, taking out the trash, making your bed, washing the dishes, and plenty more.

Doing chores can feel like . . . a chore. But putting them off isn't so great, either. Every time you think of them, you'll probably get a sinking feeling as you remember you still need to do them. Plus, not doing them can cause arguments with your parents.

The skills you'll practice in this chapter can help your work around your home go more smoothly. You might not always *love* your chores, but you can learn to make peace with them.

Thinking Thoughts That Help You Start

Thoughts are weightless and invisible, but they can make it a lot harder to get your chores done! Watch out for **thoughts that tell you doing chores is terrible** or that **it's unfair you have to do them**.

It's possible that these kinds of thoughts are true. For example, it's terrible if your parents make you carry heavy rocks for 12 hours straight. It's unfair if they force you to do all their work so they can watch TV and eat candy all day.

But as you know, sometimes your mind tells you things that aren't quite right. Your chores might *seem* terrible, but when you think about it some more, you realize the work itself isn't all that bad. And maybe the people who tell you to do the chores are also busy and working hard, so it's less unfair than your mind said it was.

Check out these types of thoughts that can get in the way of chores. You can circle the kinds your mind has told you. What is a more helpful way of thinking for the last type of thought?

Type of Thought	Example	Different Way of Thinking
Too hard	"Cleaning my room is terrible."	"I don't like cleaning my room, but it's not actually so hard."
Not fair	"Why do I have to clear the table—can't my parents do it?"	"Everyone is working and doing their part."
Takes too long	"It will take me forever to put away these books."	

You don't have to trick yourself into loving chores or pretend like they're your favorite thing ever. But often, you can make your work smoother and less painful by coming up with different ways of thinking about it!

Making Chores Just the Right Size

What happens inside you when your parents say these kinds of things?

"Clean your room."

"Put away your toys."

"Clear the table."

"Water the garden."

It's not surprising if you think, "Oh no!" and feel like it's too much to do. Maybe your toys are everywhere, and it seems like it'll take all day to put them away. Or your room looks like a *tornado* hit it, with clothes and toys and books everywhere.

Doing chores is a great time to use your skill of **turning a big job into a few little jobs**.

For example, Ella had to clean her room before her sleepover. At first, she felt lost and didn't know where to start. But then she broke the work into smaller steps.

Clothes
Books
Toys
Markers

Think of a chore you often need to do. How could you turn it into smaller steps that feel pretty easy? No step is too small if it helps you get moving!

Big chore:					
Smaller steps:					

Once you've broken it down, it's time to take the first step, as we'll see next.

Planning to Take the First Step

Getting started is usually the hardest part of doing chores. Before you begin, you still have the whole job to do, and it's easy to think about how much you'll hate doing it.

It's like trying to push a giant ball. It takes extra *energy* to get the ball rolling. Once it's moving, it's easier to keep it going, just like once you start a chore it's usually easier to keep working.

Here are a few ways to take that first step.

Make the first step even smaller if you need to:

Do you need to break down your first step into 2 or 3 steps?

Choose a time to do it:

When will you start?
_____ a.m./p.m.

Focus on just the first step:

Imagine the only thing you have to do is step 1. Right now, that's it!

See how much you can do in 5 minutes:

Set a timer and repeat as many times as you need to until the job is done!

Bringing Your Whole Self to the Task

So far, we've looked at how to make chores less painful: thinking about them differently, breaking them into smaller pieces, making it easier to get started.

Now let's look at what might be the most powerful tool of all. **Maybe chores don't have to be something boring or annoying.**

You can see for yourself if that's true by taking a closer look at what they actually are as you do them.

All you need to do is *notice* what it's really like to do your chore.

For example, Maria felt the running water as she rinsed her dishes after breakfast, and the smoothness of the bowl as she put it in the dishwasher.

She had always hated when her parents told her to clean her dishes, but when she looked for what she hated, she couldn't really find anything!

The great thing about this skill is that you don't need to try to change how you feel! Your feelings can be what they are.

All you're doing is noticing: **What is actually happening right now?** The box to the right lists several things you can pay attention to.

Choose one chore and think of 3 things you can notice while you do it.

> ## Things to notice during chores:
>
> - What you see
> - How your body moves
> - Sounds around you
> - Feelings in your hands
> - Your own breath

Chore: _____

Things to notice:

1 _____

2 _____

3 _____

Rewarding Yourself for a Job Well Done

There's one more skill you can use to help yourself finish your chores: **Promise yourself a little reward at the end!**

It doesn't have to be a big deal, and you definitely don't need to go out and buy anything! Even something small can keep you moving toward your goal.

It's fun to make a game of it. Lexi wanted to read her new graphic novel, but she needed to clean her room.

She decided to read one chapter after every 10 minutes of cleaning. Once she was finished, she could read as much as she wanted to!

There are limitless ways to reward yourself—just pick something you enjoy doing.

Henry chose to pet his dog for a few minutes once he finished weeding the garden bed.

Alice looked forward to creating one of her drawings after she took the food waste out to the compost bin.

Kayla couldn't wait to play in the backyard when her chores were done.

One tip: Choose things that don't involve a parent. That way you can reward yourself even if they aren't around, and you won't need them to drive you somewhere or buy you anything.

Think about things you could look forward to when you finish your work.

What are 3 ways you might reward yourself?

Ways to reward myself:

1 _____

2 _____

3 _____

CHAPTER 18

Finding It Hard to Focus

☐ Home-
   work
☐ Clean
   room

Has an adult ever told you that you need to "be more focused?" Maybe it was a parent who wanted you to do your homework, a coach giving instructions to your team, or a tutor trying to help you learn. You might have even said it to yourself!

No matter who the message comes from, it takes more than *wanting* to focus to make it happen. Simply trying harder rarely works and may lead to more conflict and frustration.

In this chapter, you'll build the skills that can help you stay on target. With the right tools, it will be easier to focus and do what you need to do.

Shrinking Your Focus from Big to Small

Have you ever tried to focus on many things at the same time? It's like trying to read a whole page at once—pretty impossible!

When it's time to focus, go small. Narrow your attention to just what you need to do right now. You can find your smaller focus by using the task breakdown from chapter 3. Then give what you're doing as much of your awareness as you can.

Lots of good things happen when you make this shift.

You feel less anxiety. You know exactly what you're working on. You're less afraid it will go badly because you can see what needs to be done.

You're also not worrying about everything else you'll need to do.

It's easier to get started. Less anxiety also means it's easier to take that first important step.

When you know just what to do, there's less stopping you from doing it!

You're less likely to be distracted. A smaller focus means it's easier for your mind to settle into what you're doing instead of bouncing from one thing to another.

Less distraction allows your work to be faster and easier!

Once you know just what you're going to work on, it's good to create a clean space for doing it, as you'll see on the next page.

Clearing Away Things That Distract You

The more you have around you when you're trying to work, the harder it is to focus. When your eyes land on something close by, it's easy to get distracted.

It's even easier to get pulled away by other things if you're not loving the task you're doing! It's almost like the mind is looking for ways to escape.

Take a look at the area where you do your work, such as a desk or a table. Write in the box below any things that get in the way of your focus that might be good to put somewhere else.

Things that make it harder to focus:

_____

_____

_____

When you sit down to work, take a minute to make the area nice and tidy.

Put away items you won't need while you work. Take special care to remove the things you know will pull you away, such as games or screens.

If you switch tasks, keep only the things you'll be using and clear away the rest. For example, if you switch from math homework to science, put away your math book and calculator.

A clear workspace helps your mind to be clear, too!

Reminding Yourself What to Do

Sometimes you might lose your focus because you simply forget what you meant to be doing.

Carter, for example, missed his school bus because he got caught up in watching a weird bug he spotted on the way to the bus stop.

It can be hard to *remember to remember* what you need to be doing! Telling yourself to remember (or someone else telling you) doesn't work very well when it's so easy to forget.

It works better to **have things that remind you what your task is**. There are many ways to remind yourself:

- Write a note to yourself and leave it where you'll see it.

- Set an alarm.

- Put the task in your calendar.

Bring trumpet home!

Reminders can be extra helpful when you have to stop what you're doing and then come back to it. For example, you might need to pause from doing your homework and use the restroom, and then come back and keep working.

It helps to set an alarm to go off in a few minutes. That way, if you forget to return to your homework, the alarm will remind you.

What might be a good way to remind yourself of something you need to do?

Ways to remind myself:

_____

_____

_____

Talking Yourself Through to Stay on Task

You can also keep yourself on track by **saying what you need to be doing as you do it**. It's like being your own coach!

For example, you can tell yourself, "I'm going upstairs to brush my teeth," so you're less likely to lose your focus along the way.

It's helpful to actually **say the words out loud** if possible. When you do, you're giving yourself a stronger reminder than if you just think it to yourself. Speaking is also harder to interrupt than thinking is.

Carter used this skill to coach himself to the bus on time. "I'm walking to my bus," he said. "It leaves at 7:30. I'm going straight there."

However, it doesn't always work to say things out loud, like if you're in church or at the library. At those times, you can talk silently or just think the words to yourself.

When might you use this tool to help yourself stay on task?

I could talk myself through tasks when I:

_____

_____

_____

_____

_____

See how it works for you, and have fun being your own coach!

Becoming an Active Learner

Research has shown that our attention starts to drift after 10 to 15 minutes, or even less if we really struggle with focus. But your classes are *much* longer than 10 minutes! So of course your mind is going to wander in class.

You'll find that it's easier to pay attention when you take an active role in the classroom. Here's how to practice being an **active learner**!

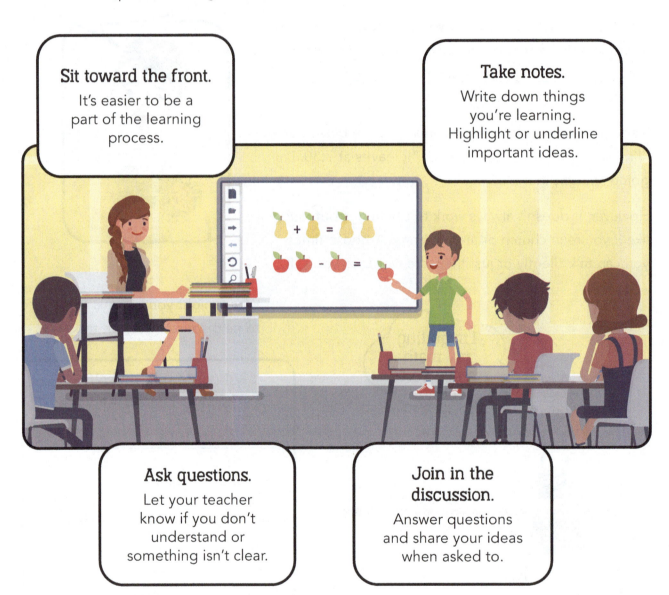

Sit toward the front.
It's easier to be a part of the learning process.

Take notes.
Write down things you're learning. Highlight or underline important ideas.

Ask questions.
Let your teacher know if you don't understand or something isn't clear.

Join in the discussion.
Answer questions and share your ideas when asked to.

You can try out some of these things like a scientist. Do an experiment to see what happens when you use these practices compared to being less active. Find the behaviors that are helpful and use them often!

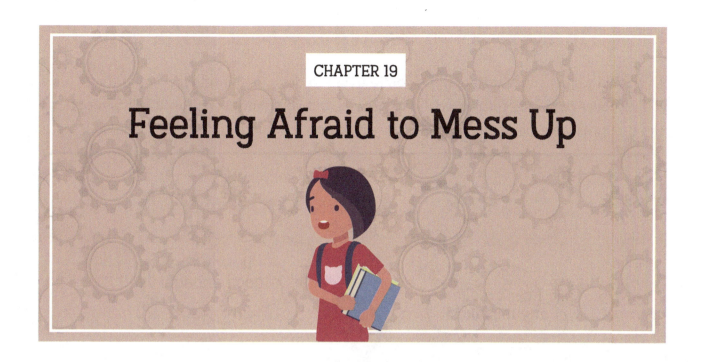

Feeling Afraid to Mess Up

CHAPTER 19

It's good to want to do things well. If good is good, then perfect must be better . . . right? It might seem like it—if only perfect were possible! But perfect has a way of staying just beyond our reach.

Trying hard to make things perfect takes so much time and work. You can still do a great job and also let it be imperfect. In fact, you'll probably do things better when you're able to let go of perfection.

Read on to discover how to do your best while aiming for less than perfect. It might be hard at first. But with practice, you'll start to see how good can actually be *better* than perfect!

Thinking Better Thoughts About Perfection

It's normal to feel some anxiety when you're trying to do something that's hard or that you've never done before. You want it to go well, but you're not sure how it will turn out. The thoughts your mind tells you can make things even harder!

These kinds of thoughts lead to more anxiety. They also have a way of blocking you from doing your work, since you're afraid that anything you do won't be good enough.

When you look more closely at these thoughts, you'll find they probably aren't true.

- Perfect isn't possible.

- It's okay to make mistakes.

- You can control your *effort*, not the outcome.

What is a thought you've had about needing to do something perfectly?

_____

_____

You can use your **Realize, Research, Revise** skills from chapter 2 to see if this thought is right, and if there's a more helpful way of thinking.

Making a Plan for Doing It Imperfectly

Since perfect isn't possible, a better goal is to **aim for imperfect**. Why? Because it's always going to be less than perfect! There's no perfect email message, art project, essay, or handwriting. So you may as well aim for where you're always going to end up!

And of course, "imperfect" doesn't mean bad. It can mean good, or even *great*. You can plan for imperfect and still work hard and have high standards.

You can keep aiming for the bullseye, even though you'll probably never hit the very exact center of the target. Even a slightly off-center bullseye is still a bullseye!

Once you have this useful goal in mind, you can plan for how you'll complete your task. Use your task breakdown skill to **create small, easy steps**, keeping in mind that none of them has to be perfect.

It's great to include when you'll finish each step as part of your planning. Trying to be perfect usually takes more time than you have. Setting time limits will help you keep moving toward being done.

You can come back to helpful thoughts if your mind tells you to spend more time on a step when you really need to move on.

Remind yourself that the goal is *good*, and that you have enough time for good but not for perfect.

What are some helpful thoughts you can tell yourself to keep moving toward your goal of imperfectly done?

I can tell myself:

_____

_____

_____

_____

_____

_____

Letting Go of Past and Future

When you're afraid that what you're working on won't be good enough, the fear is about the future: the grade you'll get, what someone will think, how it's going to turn out.

Your mind might also look back at times in the past—maybe when something didn't go well, or when you made a mistake. Those times can make you fear that you'll **have the same disappointments all over again**.

But you can't control the future. All you can control is what you do right now.

You can't change the past. Whatever happened has already happened.

What kinds of thoughts have you had about the past or future that can make you think your work has to be perfect?

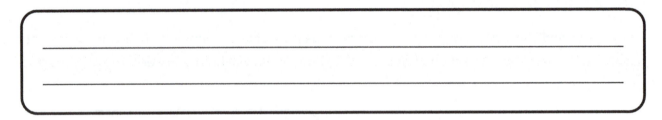

When you notice that your thoughts are drifting away from what's happening right now, welcome yourself back to where you *actually are*.

Take a breath in and say to yourself, "Just."

Breathe out and say, "Now."

Just now. This is where you are. This is what you're doing. This is where you can do your beautiful imperfect work.

You have what you need to handle this very moment. You've got this!

IV. Managing Relationships

CHAPTER 20

Having Conflict with a Friend

Friends can be one of the best things in your life . . . and sometimes one of the most difficult! At some point, friends will disagree, and the conflict can get intense.

Getting through a rough patch with a friend takes skills: being assertive, working with thoughts, careful problem-solving. At times, you might decide to stop being friends with someone, like if they don't respect your feelings and aren't willing to work things out.

But for the many friendships that are worth keeping, working through an argument is one of the most valuable things you can do. It can help you not only solve the conflict but even build a stronger friendship.

Checking Unhelpful Thoughts About Your Friend

Feeling upset at a friend can change how you see them. For example, Clara usually thought of her friend Lola as someone who was kind and fun to be with. But when they had an argument about which game to play, Lola looked a lot different to Clara.

"She's annoying and bossy," Clara's mind told her. "And she's no fun to play with."

These thoughts made Clara feel angrier at Lola. She even started to think that maybe she didn't want to be friends with Lola anymore.

Think of a conflict you've had with a friend you like. In what ways did it change how you thought about them?

_____

_____

Clara wasn't so sure her thoughts about Lola were right when she took a closer look at them. Sure, she was annoyed with her friend about their argument. And Lola *did* get bossy about it. But that's not what she was like most of the time.

When Clara thought about it some more, she had to admit that *she'd* been a little bossy, too. And Lola probably thought Clara was being just as annoying!

Clara was able to come up with a different way of thinking that was more true and helpful.

"Lola is fun to be with most of the time," she realized. "But I don't like it when we argue." That new way of thinking made it easier to work things out with her friend.

You can use your **Realize, Research, Revise** skills to see if your thoughts about a friend are right. Sometimes they will be, and you'll have friendships you even decide to end.

But a lot of the time, you'll discover better ways of thinking that help you to work through the problem, and even **find a solution that's a win-win**!

Finding a Win-Win with Your Friend

The best outcome of a conflict with your friend is that **you both win**. They get what they want, and so do you.

Maybe neither of you gets *everything* you wanted, but you both can feel good about how you worked things out.

Think of a disagreement you've had with a friend. It could be one you're still having or one you've solved. Briefly describe it in the box below.

There are many ways to find a win-win solution. Think of one that sounds okay to you and that will seem fair to your friend. Making a win-win plan can help when it comes time to do the actual working-it-out with your friend.

Your solution will include a win for you and a win for your friend. Here's how to tell if it's fair: Imagine that your friend could pick either their "win" or your "win." Would you be just as happy with *either* choice, or does one still feel more like winning?

> **Our conflict:**
> _____
> _____
> _____
> _____

If the options feel uneven, see if you're able to make them more equal. When you come up with a solution, you can write it in the box below.

> **Our win-win solution:**
> _____
> _____
> _____

The best win-win result is that you and your friend are still friends after this conflict.

You might even have a stronger bond after working it out together.

Making a Plan to Solve the Conflict

When you're ready to work things out with your friend, it helps to have an idea of how you'll do it. One of the first things to decide is if you and your friend are feeling calm enough to talk about it. It's fine if you still have strong feelings! But if either of you is so upset that you're not ready to talk, you can wait for another time.

Once you're ready, you can follow these steps to **reach a solution that works for both of you**.

1 Understand your friend's side of things.

Ask your friend to tell you their thoughts and feelings about the conflict. Give them time to tell you, without interrupting them. Check to be sure you really understand.

2 Tell your friend how you think and feel.

Use "I" statements to share your thoughts and feelings. For example, Clara told Lola, "I felt angry when you said my game was stupid."

What do you want to say to your friend about what happened?

> I would tell my friend that:
>
> I feel _____
> _____
> I think _____
> _____

3 Come up with possible solutions.

Think with your friend about ways to resolve the conflict that would meet *both* of your needs (win-win).

4 Choose a solution.

Find one of the options you came up with that works for both of you. Check to see that your friend feels okay about this solution. Check in with yourself, too, to make sure it feels all right.

If you're not sure the solution works, you and your friend can always go back to steps 1 and 2.

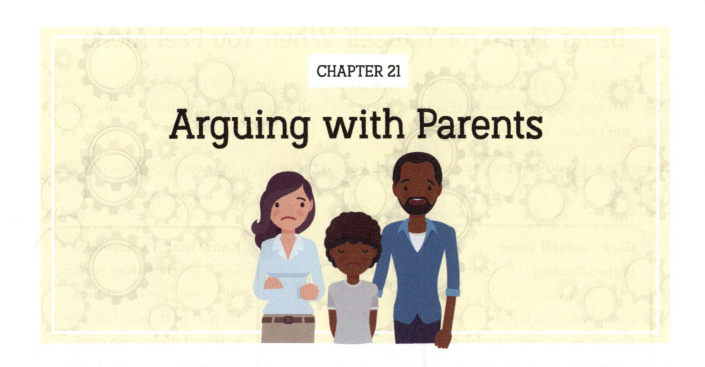

CHAPTER 21

Arguing with Parents

Sometimes the hardest conflict of all is with your parents. Arguments with them can feel unfair because they're bigger and have a lot more power, and they might overreact because they're tired or hungry.

Conflict can happen when you want to do something but they say no, or they tell you to do something that you don't want to. You and your parents will also have different ideas about what is safe or what you're old enough to do.

You can't get rid of all conflict with parents, and it wouldn't even be good if you could. Conflict is part of how your relationship with them grows and changes as you get older and gain more control over your life.

Arguments with your parents will never be comfortable, but with practice, they can be less painful and even help you understand each other better.

Being There for Yourself When You Feel Alone

It can be painful to be on the outs with your parents. You might feel like you're all alone and you can't turn to your mom or dad for support. It's also a lonely feeling when it seems like they don't understand you.

In hard times, **you can be your own friend**. Follow these steps to show yourself some kindness.

1 **Give yourself some understanding.** Let yourself know that *yes, this is hard*. It's okay to feel big feelings, like anger at your parents or sadness for yourself. Make space for whatever it's like for you right now.

2 **Know that it's normal.** Every child has had conflict with their parents at times. It's part of the deal between kids and those who care for them. You're not really alone in this experience. You're fully part of what it means to be human.

3 **Be the Observer of thoughts and feelings.** You're willing to feel your emotions, and yet you're not turning *into* your emotions! You're still you, and the things you think and feel are just part of your experience. Observe them, and as you do, notice how there's a part of you that's aware of them without being changed by them.

These three steps make up **self-compassion**, an incredibly helpful skill to develop.

Having compassion for yourself means you *see* that you're hurting, and you do what you can to **help yourself feel less alone and upset**.

Trying Out New Ways of Seeing Things

Sometimes the mind's tricks show up when you and your parents disagree. That doesn't mean your parents are always right! But these tricks can make things harder than they have to be.

That's what happened when Evan wanted to have his friend over for a sleepover, but his mom and dad said it wasn't a good idea because he had a swim meet early the next morning.

Evan's thoughts were making him feel more and more upset. Can you spot the trick his mind was using?

"My parents never understand me! I can't do anything fun with my friends!"

When Evan looked closer at his thoughts, he saw that he *did* get to do some fun things with his friends, even though his parents said no to a sleepover. And they might not understand him this time, but a lot of the time they do.

Evan realized his mind was using **All-or-Nothing Thinking**. He still didn't agree with his parents, but he was able to see things more clearly.

When was a time your mind played a trick on you during an argument with your parents?

Argument	Thought	Mind Trick

Changing your thinking doesn't mean you always need to agree with your parents! Holding different beliefs from them is a really important part of growing up.

At the same time, it can help to try out new ways of seeing things. It's easier to work out the conflict when your mind isn't playing tricks on you!

Being Assertive with Parents

When your parents are upset, you might feel like they're not hearing you. It's true that parents don't always listen! They aren't perfect, and sometimes they react without thinking, assume things that aren't true, or cut you off when you're trying to explain. It can seem like there's no use trying to tell them how you feel.

But most of the time, they probably *want* to hear your side of things. They want to know why something they said hurt your feelings, or what feels unfair about not letting you do something.

When your parents are willing to, talk with them about your thoughts and feelings. It's easier to talk things through when you and your parents are less upset so you're able to hear each other more clearly.

They might change their minds based on what you tell them. But even if they don't, it can feel good just to know you stood up for yourself and said things that were important to you.

It's most useful to talk about how *you* feel, rather than telling your parents what's wrong with *them*. For example, if Lisa told her parents, "You're mean, and you never listen!" they might just tell her that's not true. But it's harder for them to disagree if Lisa says, "I don't like it when you interrupt me."

Part of being assertive is also trying to understand how your parents see things. You don't have to agree with them, but it's helpful to know where they're coming from.

Think of a recent argument with your parents. What thoughts and feelings would you like to share with them?

_____

_____

CONGRATULATIONS!

Well done working your way through this book!

The time and energy you've put in here will keep paying off as you use your new skills to handle hard things. Your future self will thank you!

Sometimes you'll find that you need more practice, and that is 100% okay. Remember, we're aiming for progress, not perfection. 😆 Just keep this workbook somewhere handy so it's easy to find when you need it.

We're wishing you health, happiness, and lots of fun in the days and years ahead. We'll see you back here as often as you pick up this book!

About the Authors

Seth J. Gillihan, PhD, is a licensed psychologist, podcast host, and creator of the *Think Act Be* online school. He specializes in evidence-based mindful cognitive behavioral therapy (CBT) for depression, anxiety, OCD, insomnia, and related conditions.

Seth is the best-selling author of several books, including *Mindful Cognitive Behavioral Therapy*; the *CBT Deck for Kids and Teens* (co-authored with his daughter Ada); *The CBT Deck*; *The CBT Deck for Anxiety, Rumination, and Worry*; *The CBT Flip Chart*; *A Mindful Year* (co-author); *Cognitive Behavioral Therapy Made Simple*; and *Retrain Your Brain*.

Seth served on the faculty in the psychiatry department at the University of Pennsylvania and taught full-time in the psychology department at Haverford College. He has co-authored over forty book chapters and peer-reviewed research articles, and has presented his research nationally and internationally. He lives near Philadelphia with his wife and three kids.

...

Ada J. L. Gillihan enjoyed working with her dad again to create another tool for young people. She knows what it's like to go through a rough patch, as she experienced a couple years of intense anxiety in second and third grades. Although it hasn't completely gone away, it has gotten so much better with the help of therapy, CBT, and the love and support of her family. Ada enjoys sewing, guinea pigs, music, and spending time with her friends.

...

Faye L. L. Gillihan had fun helping her dad make a CBT workbook just for kids. She has always liked CBT exercises and enjoys combining words and pictures in a way that is visually pleasing and easy to understand. Her favorite hobby is writing, which she tries to do in most of her free time. Faye also reads loads of books and is open to reading suggestions. She hopes that everyone will learn from CBT and is eager and excited to make more tools with her father (and maybe sister) in the future.

Made in the USA
Monee, IL
20 December 2024

74946483R00103